GREENWICH LIBRARY
BOOK SALE

50p

D0272670

SQUIRRELS

SQUIRRELS

•JESSICA HOLM•

with illustrations by
GUY TROUGHTON

Whittet Books

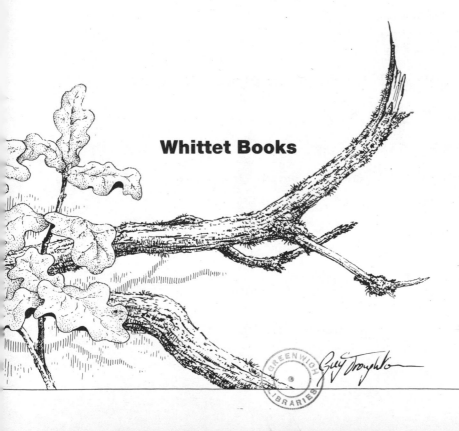

GREENWICH LIBRARIES

Endpaper illustration: red and grey squirrels in winter (for identification, see p.33).

GREENWICH LIBRARIES EL ✗ LOC

INV

15-3-93 £6.95

ACC NO 3 8028 01198851 3

CAT 599.3232

First published 1987
Reprinted 1990
Text © 1987 by Jessica Holm
Illustrations © 1987 by Guy Troughton
Whittet Books Ltd, 18 Anley Road, London W14 0BY

Design by Richard Kelly

All rights reserved

British Library Cataloguing in Publication Data

Holm, Jessica
  Squirrels.
    1. Squirrels—Great Britain
    2. Mammals—Great Britain
    I. Title
    599.32'32   QL737.R68

    ISBN 0–905483–55–3

Typeset by Inforum Ltd, Portsmouth.

Printed and bound by Biddles of Guildford.

Contents

Preface

I cannot claim to have been fascinated by squirrels all my life. I very much wanted to work on red deer, but that was not to be. One muggy July, fresh from the anti-climax of graduation, I went on safari to the Glenbranter hills in Scotland in search of deer, experience, and, who knows, maybe even a job. Having been eaten alive by mosquitoes, trudged up and down a lot of forestry rides, and had the fear of God put into me about the dreaded 'immobilon' (a powerful drug used to sedate deer for the purposes of radio tagging; doesn't hurt the deer, but has quite staggering effects upon us humans), I didn't end up seeing any deer. But I did gain some experience. Mainly regarding what a smashing breed mammalogists are, confirming the fact that I passionately wanted to work in the field. Ultimately I did get a job, only not working with deer, but with squirrels instead. If anybody had told me as an undergraduate that I would devote thousands of hours, indeed years, to the study of squirrels, I would probably just have laughed.

It was then that I first became aware of the red/grey scenario. Everywhere I went, and regardless of who I spoke to, stories of the red and the grey squirrel were legion. It seems that everyone has his or her own answer to why greys have 'taken over', but when I searched the literature, answers only pointed to more questions.

Many of those questions have still not been answered, and there is a great deal more finding out about squirrels still to be done. It's hard to beat the natural history observations of Middleton in the 1930s and Monica Shorten in the 1950s, of such quality were their accounts. And yet since their time there has been a wealth of equally diligent investigation into the details of the biology of these two squirrel species, culminating in an effort to understand how grey squirrels have managed so effectively to replace our native reds. This is the question that plagues modern squirrelologists, and I have no doubt that we will be kept busy for many years yet trying to unravel the answer. Sorting out the squirrel story certainly provides any mammalogist with sufficient challenge for a lifetime's work.

This book sets out to shed light on a few of your questions, and to help you to better understand these delightful creatures with whom you might share your local wood, your garden, or even your window sill. I am certain that I will not be able to answer all of your questions, we still have so much to learn about squirrels. But I do hope that you will find my account interesting and informative. I am sure that many of you will have things to add, many will have first-hand experience of the animals, but I hope that there will be something new for everyone. After all, despite all their misdemeanours, I have yet to meet a soul who can only speak ill of squirrels.

Royal Holloway and Bedford New College   *October 1986*

Acknowledgments

I think that this is about the most difficult part of this book that I will have to write. I am bound to leave somebody really important out ... so I apologize in advance, 'really important person' ... you know who you are.

Firstly, soppy as it might seem, I have to thank my mother and stepfather. Still living in hope that I might get 'a proper job', they were extremely tolerant of my bedroom full of beasties, even if skinning a badger on the kitchen table did prove to be too much of a test! I was first bitten specifically by the 'mammal bug' when I went to Royal Holloway College, and was taught by Pat Morris. I am eternally grateful to him for his time, patience and humour. He is truly one of the most helpful people that I have ever met, and without him, I doubt that I would ever have been in a position to write any of this.

Once I had plumped for squirrels, there are various folk that helped me along the way, and to whom I am grateful. Firstly, to the late Judy Rowe, who introduced me to squirrels, via red deer, and to my first job. She was a wonderfully strong character, and instilled in me a feeling of independence that I would now be lost without. I am grateful also to Robert and Bridget Kenward and to the staff of ITE Monks Wood who remember me, with whom I worked out my squirrel apprenticeship after graduation. Moving from grey squirrel research to red, I must thank Melody Tonkin, Jonathan Reynolds and John Gurnell, squirrelologists before me, and always ready to chat about them. Thanks also to John for reading this text.

I started work on the Isle of Wight in 1983, and the first person that I must thank is Mr Norman Groves, my bank manager. Never have I met such an understanding and tolerant man ... please don't ever retire, Mr Groves, I'd sink without you. I would also like to thank the People's Trust for Endangered Species, the Mammal Society and the World Wildlife Fund for supporting my work, and more recently, the Natural Environment Research Council and the Vincent Wildlife Trust for their support. Thank you to Frank and Maretta Heap for all the coffee, and to the National Trust and Longdown Estates for study sites.

Thanks are also due to all the friends who have helped with my project, and who have kept me sane. Particularly to Jon Cox for moral support, to Marianne and Ian for just being themselves, to Tony Fisher for providing fieldwork vehicles and for generally being a Mr Fixit, and very importantly, to my two (now sadly one) Italian Spinoni (dogs) Alf and Tet, without whom long and anti-social hours of fieldwork would be lonely and dull.

9

Evolution

As far as we know, it all started 34 million years ago, with a chap called *Protosciurus* (first squirrel). But *Protosciurus*, the oldest known tree squirrel fossil, is not really very helpful, because he looks just like any other squirrel that you might expect to see scampering about in the trees today. How he got there is still a bit of a mystery. What he does tell us is that early squirrels must have been pretty good at what squirrels do best, because their modern counterparts are no more specialized.

The start of the takeover.

About 65 million years ago, as the reign of the dinosaurs finally reached an end, some unassuming little shrew-like creatures became the ancestors of modern mammals. These early mammals had a real advantage in their unique physiology; being warm blooded (they could control their body temperature, rather than lying basking in the sun, or hidden in the shade) ideally suited them not just for life on land, but for life under all sorts of hostile environmental conditions. Unlike reptiles and birds, early mammals also possessed the ability to reproduce rapidly, making them very adaptive in a fast changing environment. Instead of leaving vulnerable embryos lying about in eggs, the mother typically retains them inside her body for protection. Once she gives birth to her young, they do not have to fend for themselves, but are nourished instead by a daily guzzle from Mum's milk bar.

These traits helped to make early mammals into jolly successful beasts, and they had soon evolved and spread out into every imaginable niche on land; some even took to the air or returned to the seas. As they adapted, they changed, and all sorts of different types of mammal began to emerge, each one specialized for a particular way of life. Amongst the most successful were the rodents which cashed in on the advantages of being mammals with astounding efficiency. These creatures are remarkable in never having attained large size, something common among other mammalian groups. There are few large rodent fossils, and the largest living rodent, the South American capybara, is only the size of a small pig. Rodents breed with renowned speed, and the combination of producing vast numbers and being small animals has left virtually no corner on earth without its full complement. Their most obvious characteristic is the famous gnawing teeth (see p.35), and indeed, the name 'rodent' comes from the Latin 'rodere' meaning to gnaw.

Although the fossil record is very sparse, it is possible to trace the beginnings of the great rodent explosion, as these very successful creatures diversified, to form the three major groups that we recognize today. These are: the *Myomorpha*, or mouse-like rodents well known for their close relationship with man; the *Hystricomorpha*, or guinea pig-like rodents; and the *Sciuromorpha* or squirrel-like rodents. The *Sciuromorpha* are considered to be the most primitive of these three groups, and include members like the peculiar mountain beaver (which isn't really a true beaver at all), the pocket gophers and proper beavers. One group evolved an agile body, with strong legs, gripping claws and a huge bushy rudder-like tail equipping them perfectly for an arboreal existence – the tree squirrels.

Some other members of the squirrel clan

There are at least 267 species of squirrel. They are spread out over the whole planet except for Australia, Polynesia, Madagascar, southern South America, and totally undesirable places like deserts and ice caps where no self-respecting squirrel would want to go anyway. You might think that they would all look roughly like our familiar British tree squirrels. However, not so. The squirrel family is varied indeed, and many look nothing like the image that the word 'squirrel' evokes.

Undoubtedly, some of the most spectacular are the nocturnal flying squirrels. The name is a bit misleading, as these creatures do not actually fly. Instead, they glide from tree to tree with the aid of two large fur-covered membranes that stretch between fore and hind feet on either side of the animal's body. As it launches itself into the air, the flying squirrel stretches out its legs, and the membranes catch the wind rather like a kite. The squirrel can steer itself with its long rudder-like tail, and will normally land upright on a tree-trunk before scampering up to the top for take-off again.

Chipmunk

Flying squirrel

Mountain beaver

Marmoset

Some other members of the squirrel clan.

In contrast to the airborne flying squirrel are the ground dwelling members of the family. The chipmunks or striped gophers have shorter, less bushy tails than tree squirrels; their tails are still very expressive. They live in burrows amongst tree roots, and, although they do climb sometimes, they remain on the ground most of the time. These animals have large cheek pouches so that they can nip out of their burrows, cram their faces full of food, and race home again for a meal, before they become someone else's. Ground squirrels are quite different from chipmunks, although they too live underground and are able to store food in cheek pouches. The largest of the ground squirrels is the souslik, whose ability to raid and store huge volumes of seed makes it a serious grain pest in Eastern Europe and Russia.

Marmots are also members of the clan that live on the ground in Europe and North America. These are short-legged, stocky animals of surprising agility, which live in very close family groups. They are also amongst the largest members of the squirrel clan, weighing in at up to 8 kg. (17½1b.). Marmots are very sociable creatures, and they seem to spend most of their time playing, grooming and grazing. However, they are always carefully watched over by a sentry who will announce the arrival of potential danger with a piercing alarm call. As the winter approaches, marmots get very fat, and dig a burrow in which to hibernate. They remain in their burrows throughout the cold alpine winter, and usually mate before coming to the

African pygmy squirrel

Malabar giant squirrel

Red squirrel

The biggest, the smallest and the cutest tree squirrel.

surface again for the brief summer. Often only the dominant female in the colony will breed, all the other females acting as ranks of babysitters once the young become active.

Although the true tree squirrels are all roughly the same shape, with a cylindrical body, short fore and long hind limbs, and the inimitable bushy tail, they do come in a variety of different sizes and colours. One of the smallest is the tiny African pigmy squirrel (*Myosciurus pumilio*) weighing only 10 g. (under ½oz.). At the opposite extreme is the Indian giant or Malabar squirrel (*Ratufa indica*) weighing about 3 kg. (6½1b.). You wouldn't want that dropping out of a tree on you! Colour variations within and between species are boundless. The Malabar squirrel can vary from a deep red through all shades to striking black with tan markings. Many forest species, particularly those of far-off Thailand, are famed for their fantastic colour variations, which range through pure white, black, red, and combinations of all of these colours. There are even some green squirrels.

The amazing prairie dog

One of the most famous members of the squirrel family is the prairie dog, so-called by the American trappers because of its yelping and barking. To look at one, and see the way it lives, it is very hard to imagine that it is related to tree squirrels; in fact it would be difficult to find anything more different. Prairie dogs live on the ground in America in huge

The amazing prairie dog.

colonies called 'towns'. Each town consists of a series of burrows containing the individual dens of as many as fifteen animals. It must get pretty stuffy down there, but prairie dogs are not stupid. The burrow has an entrance and an exit, and the entrance hole is surrounded by a mound. This mound serves as a post for the colony's sentry to keep a look out, but more importantly, it creates a difference in the levels at which the entrance and exit holes emerge to air. This causes a draught and sucks air through the burrow system to ventilate it. Clever, aren't they?

Squirrels or tree rats?

We have two squirrel species in this country, the red squirrel, whose Latin name is Sciurus vulgaris, and the grey squirrel, Sciurus carolinensis. As you can see, they both belong to the same genus, Sciurus; so you can forget any stories about the grey squirrel being an impostor, nothing but a tree rat. Both species are true tree squirrels. Aristotle first used the word Sciurus, borrowed from the Greek word 'skiouros', meaning 'shade-tail'. In Britain, the word 'squirrel' was first used in the writings of St Hugh in about 1200, and by the 15th century there were many dialect words in existence such as 'scorel' or 'squerel' used in East Anglia, 'scug' used in northern English counties, and 'skuyrell' recorded in Perthshire.

Squirrels in Britain

Squirrels in the past

Fossil bones in caves (like natural pitfall traps) have shown that an animal very like our red squirrel but called White's Squirrel (*Sciurus whitei*) was present in the coniferous forests that covered Britain some 12 million years ago. The first remains of our own red squirrel (*Sciurus vulgaris*) originate from some time just before the land connection with Europe disappeared, about 7,000 – 10,000 years ago, at the end of the last Ice Age.

In recorded history, there does not appear to be any mention of another species of squirrel native to the British Isles. However, in 1781, a naturalist named Pennant described for the first time the bleached tails of British red squirrels in summer coat (probably not noticed before because red squirrels are so difficult to observe in broadleaved woodland during the summertime). In 1792 Kerr defined the British sub-species *Sciurus vulgaris leucourus*, separated purely by virtue of its light tail. We now recognize some seventeen sub-species of the red squirrel (*Sciurus vulgaris*) throughout its range, and those closest to the British Isles include *S. vulgaris vulgaris* from Southern Scandinavia, *S.vulgaris varius* from Arctic Sandinavia, and *S. vulgaris fuscoater* from north-west Europe. These sub-species are really very similar to look at, and they interbreed readily in captivity, making them difficult to define. Indeed, there are historical records of foreign squirrels being imported to London markets for sale as pets, particularly during the eighteenth century, and it may well be that the enormous colour variation that we see amongst British red squirrels today (see p.28) is at least partly due to interbreeding between introduced sub-species and our own British red squirrels, but this is by no means certain.

In Ireland, the first records of red squirrels were of specimens sadly stripped of their skins in about 1243, and in Wales similar hunting records exist from the 13th century. It is difficult to know if this means that there were squirrels living in Welsh and Irish woodlands, or if the skins were simply imported from other countries. However, it would appear that in the 15th century, red squirrels disappeared completely from Irish soil, and were not reintroduced again until the early 19th century. Why did they disappear? It seems that industry (fuel for factories), agriculture and war made enormous demands on the timber resources of the countryside, and forest destruction took place on quite a dramatic scale. In Wales and Scotland there is a similar story. Red squirrel numbers declined rapidly during the acute timber shortage of the 15th and 16th centuries, and during the 18th century the Scottish red squirrels were all but extinct. They were not the only animals to suffer as a result of man's need for timber, for it was during this period that the splendid forest-dwelling capercaillie became extinct in Britain.

In England, there was similar de-forestation, but red squirrels did not seem to suffer so badly. At the beginning of the 19th century, everybody started to plant trees, especially fast-growing conifers, to replace the ancient broadleafed woodlands that had been felled. Red squirrels recovered in these new woodlands, and by the beginning of this century, they had reached peak numbers. In 1889, 2,281 red squirrels were shot by the commissioners of the New Forest, as timber pests, and in 1903, the Highland Squirrel Club was formed, proudly announcing the destruction of 82,000 red squirrels in its first thirty years of existence.

The Highland Squirrel Club.

In 1876, a Mr Brocklehurst set the scene for today's British squirrel story when he released a pair of North American grey squirrels into Henbury Park in Cheshire. This hobby soon caught on, because people liked the look of the 'new' squirrels, and old Mr Brocklehurst started a trend for introduction that was to continue for nearly fifty years, long after their harmful effects were beginning to be realized. Of 33 known introductions of grey squirrels (even one reported from South Africa), only one failed to establish.

17

The best known introductions were made at Woburn Park, the first of which took place in 1889. Grey squirrels spread particularly well from Woburn, and just to make sure that they did, many Woburn greys were shipped all over the place at the turn of the century, even to Regent's Park in London.

So, in the early 1900s, we had native red squirrels at plague proportions, and the beginnings of a grey squirrel population in Britain. What happened next?

Red v grey : the unsolved mystery

Between 1900 and 1925, red squirrel numbers declined drastically all over the British Isles. They stopped culling in the New Forest in 1927, and heaven knows what happened to the Highland Squirrel Club. Why the decline? It is still a commonly held belief that the grey invaders drove out red squirrels by chasing and killing adults, driving them out of their dreys, and killing red squirrel litters. It is true that there have been recorded sightings of aggression between the two species, and even of grey squirrels killing young reds, but it would seem that greys are just as likely to chase and kill their own kind as they are to persecute reds.

It's tough being a red squirrel.

Epidemic disease is also thought to have had a serious effect upon red squirrel numbers during this century. Coccidiosis is a disease caused by a gut parasite called *Eimeria sciuorum* and certainly many of the dead and dying red squirrels were found to have this disease. More worrying was the presence of another disease called parapoxvirus, with symptoms not unlike myxomatosis, which is found in rabbits.

Was the grey squirrel responsible for the disease amongst native reds? No, it wasn't. Out of 44 districts where red squirrels were affected by disease between 1900 and 1920, only 4 had grey squirrels present. Indeed, at about the same time, the surge in grey squirrel numbers spreading out from release sites also suffered a temporary setback due to a coccidiosis outbreak. But grey squirrels did not seem to be affected by the more serious parapoxvirus. It is thought that this disease may be stress related, and this would certainly account for the susceptibility of reds; already under pressure from the grey invasion, local red squirrels were probably suffering from overcrowding and possibly food shortages. Although it is difficult to establish exactly how the disease works, this is a valid theory and deserves further investigation. Add to this a bit of bad weather, and somebody chopping down your wood, and you have a perfect recipe for a very stressed squirrel.

This disease epidemic could not have come at a worse time for red squirrels. They suffered a terrible decline, exacerbated by further demands on the country's timber resources during the two world wars, and a series of vicious winters between 1939 and 1943. Not hampered in the same way by the parapoxvirus illness, and better able to survive in the small broadleaved woodlands left after planted conifers had been felled for wartime use, grey squirrels expanded their numbers enormously. The British tree squirrel niche (that is, the place in the eco-system for a medium-sized tree-dwelling seed-eater) was being filled by a larger and more numerous species, seemingly much more successful and able to replace our native red squirrel completely. The questions of how and why this replacement occurred are obviously very long and complex to answer, and we still don't understand all the relevant points. The only certain thing seems to be that greys are becoming more widely established and at the same time our red squirrel population is fading away.

One approach would be to look for evidence of competition. If the two species relate to their environment in slightly different ways, that is, they use its resources (nest sites, food, etc.) differently, one strategy may prove to be more efficient than the other, thus creating a competitive situation, with a winner and a loser. What we must try to do is to understand the way in

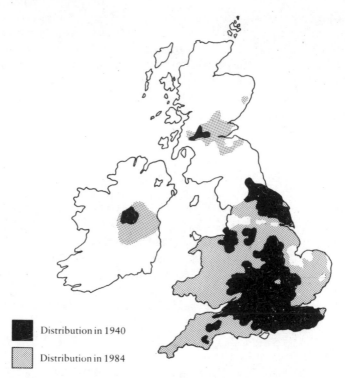

Distribution in 1940

Distribution in 1984

Past and present distribution of grey squirrels in the British Isles.

which that interaction works, so that we can ensure our native red squirrels never completely lose the battle for survival.

Squirrels in the present

Maps showing the distributions of red and grey squirrels are almost mirror images of one another. Where the grey squirrel is, the red is not. From countrywide abundance in the early 1900s, red squirrels have now become so scarce that most young folk in the South have never seen one. On the other hand, with less than a century of British citizenship, grey squirrels are now so common that when you mention the word 'squirrel', it is a grey chap that springs to most people's minds.

If you wanted to see a red squirrel these days, most of you would have a long journey. The most recent distribution maps shown here are probably already out of date, and red squirrel range will have contracted even further by the time this book is published. Grey squirrels on the other hand have

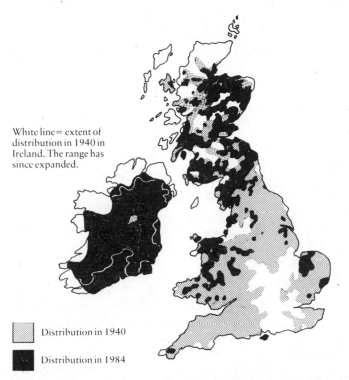

White line = extent of distribution in 1940 in Ireland. The range has since expanded.

Distribution in 1940

Distribution in 1984

Past and present distribution of red squirrels in the British Isles.

extended their range enormously from the original points of introduction. Initially checked by natural barriers like unsuitable countryside, rivers and areas of industrial development, the resourceful grey, a great traveller and not averse to the odd dip, has nevertheless managed to spread well. Grey squirrels are now common throughout most of England and Wales, and are fast establishing themselves in Scotland. In Ireland, greys have spread rapidly from Dublin (where they most probably arrived by boat with tails held aloft to catch the breeze – see p.119) and the introduction site at Castle Forbes in Longford, to gain a firm hold in many central and northern counties.

Red squirrels do take refuge on a number of islands. On Anglesey they were not safe from grey invasion, due to the existence of a road bridge. Safer isles include Skye, and most notably the south coast islands of Brownsea and the Isle of Wight. There are now no red squirrels in southern and central England at all, and those on the Isle of Wight particularly represent an

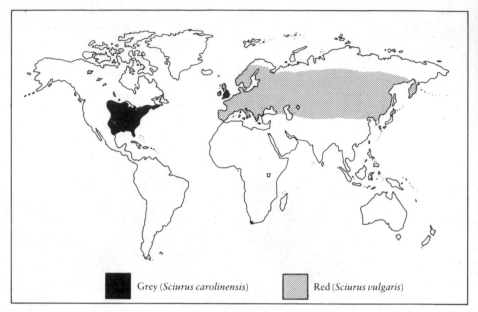

| Grey (*Sciurus carolinensis*) | Red (*Sciurus vulgaris*) |

Worldwide distribution of red and grey squirrels.

isolated but viable population that should be protected at all costs.

It is very interesting that red squirrels seem to have retreated into the massive areas of planted conifer found commonly in Scotland and northern England. Could it be that they are better able to withstand invasion by grey squirrels when living in the type of forest in which they evolved prior to the last Ice Age? Grey squirrels have certainly advanced apace through our lowland broadleaf woodlands, replacing the reds as they go. It is worth remembering that grey squirrels have lived in broadleaved woodland for millions of years (as opposed to only a few thousand years in the case of British reds), so reds may prefer conifers and greys do less well there. However, greys can live in conifers, and are already doing so at many locations all over the country.

Throughout the rest of the world, you would expect to find various sub-species of the red squirrel (*Sciurus vulgaris*) in woodlands all over Eurasia, from the Mediterranean to Northern Scandinavia, in Spain, and eastwards through the USSR to China and Korea. Grey squirrels on the other hand, hale from eastern north America. They were introduced to southern Africa at the beginning of this century, and to Great Britain between 1876 and 1929. Thus, at present, this is the only country in the world where these two species have been forced into contact by man's intervention in their natural distribution. Hopefully, the lessons that we have learned will discourage any further introductions of grey squirrels into the range of the red squirrel.

... and squirrels in the future

Are red squirrels to become extinct in Britain? It is impossible to say. There is no doubt that we are in severe danger of losing the last of our red squirrels still resident in their native habitat of broadleaf woodland. There are a few left in Cumbria, some in Scotland, Wales, East Anglia and Ireland. These populations are all vulnerable to invasion by grey squirrels, and at the moment, very little can be done to prevent the greys taking over. The Isle of Wight is probably the only place in central and southern England where you can find red squirrels in native woodland, and even here there has been talk of a road link with the mainland which might allow invasion by the grey hordes.

It seems unthinkable that we should lose red squirrels in the British Isles altogether. However, it would be prudent to glance again at the current distribution of this species in Britain (see p.21), whilst reflecting on the complete and unexplained disappearance of red squirrels from Ireland in the 15th century, and from Scotland in the 18th century. If a similar extinction were to occur now, that would be the end of red squirrels in Britain.

There is no doubt that we have to get a move on in researching the problems of red and grey squirrels. We have to accept grey squirrels as British mammals now, and conservation of red squirrels will have to be very positive. Certainly it should be a top priority to understand better the way in which these two species relate to their environment and how they might compete; what are the requirements for survival of each species and how do they differ in their ecology? There are moves within forestry organizations to adopt wildlife conservation as a secondary objective to harvesting timber, a commendable aim. We should match it with sensible management proposals for red squirrels, suggesting details of how they can be helped. Planting regimes that could best favour red squirrels are being researched, and habitat conservation will play a major role in the future of British red squirrels. It may be possible to design management techniques to favour red squirrels in woods where both species are present. For instance, supplementary feeding of reds is being investigated as a way of helping them.

It is logical that isolated populations of red squirrels should be protected at all costs. Ensuring their survival could be vital to re-introductions that may be required at some date in the future at other places.

Thus far, we have simply sat back and watched as introduced grey squirrels have become as common a sight as pigeons in Trafalgar Square. Most of us have either forgotten or never even seen a red squirrel. Certainly if we want to retain two species of British squirrel, there is going to have to be some action, and quick. Moreover, that action must be based on a real understanding of squirrels in detail – not just their ecology and behaviour, but their whole biology.

A red squirrel feeding on fallen acorns.

The squirrel's body

From the outside

Squirrels have very distinctive bodies; you are hardly likely to mistake a squirrel for anything else, largely on account of its long, plume-like tail. Most people think of a squirrel as a cute, rounded, cuddly thing, and grey squirrels are certainly quite robust, but a red squirrel on the move is a very lithe and light-weight animal, almost a long, orange, furry tube. Red squirrels weigh an average of about 300g. (10.5 oz.), whilst grey squirrels average about 520g. (18 oz.). There is no real difference between the weights of males and females, but an individual squirrel's weight can alter dramatically during the different seasons. Funnily enough, they are usually heavier in the winter when we all worry about them starving in the cold weather. It is during the sleepy, warm days of summer that the squirrel wastes away, and is more likely to die of starvation whilst we laze on some foreign beach than during a standard British freeze up (see p.90).

Legs, claws and double-jointed feet

Squirrels have short front legs, and much longer hind legs, an adaptation for leaping. The very powerful hind legs provide the thrust of the leap, and the shorter front legs act like shock absorbers to cushion the landing. You could think of them as big furry frogs. Squirrels can perform spectacular leaps of 6m. (20ft.) or more. They are not always 100 per cent confident though, and you can sometimes watch an animal sitting on a precarious perch swishing its tail and chattering wildly, trying to find the courage for take-off. Occasionally things go badly wrong, and I have watched a grey squirrel fall from about 10m. (30 ft.) up to land with a thud, then get up and scamper off having sustained a blow to the pride, but being otherwise unharmed.

The front feet have four slender toes, each with a sharp, arched claw. The thumb is reduced to a little lump used when holding food. The hind foot is much longer, with five clawed toes. Squirrel footprints in snow or mud leave a distinctive pattern, with two small front footprints placed between and slightly behind the wider, splayed hind prints. Each set of four prints is divided from the next by a gap of about 25cm. (10 inches) as the squirrel hops forwards (see p.26).

Going up and down tree-trunks is no problem at all, thanks to long, sharp claws, and double-jointed hind feet. Going up, the squirrel clasps the trunk with all four feet spread wide, and claws hooked into the bark. The front

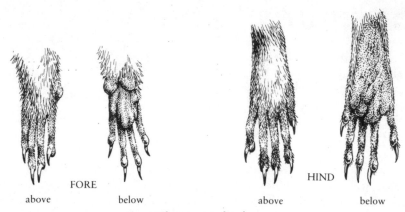

FORE   HIND

above   below   above   below

The squirrel's feet.

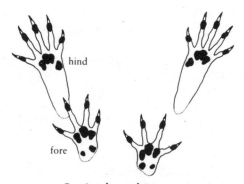

hind

fore

Squirrel tracks.

feet reach forward whilst the hind legs push up. Then the squirrel hangs on with the front feet whilst the hind legs catch up. In real life, it just looks as if the animal glides across the surface of the bark, usually spiralling round the trunk as it goes. Coming down is a really crafty business. Facing down-wards, the hind feet are stretched out behind and rotated through 180° so that the squirrel can hang upside down by its hind claws (see p.75). Otherwise the motion is much the same as going up, only gravity does all the work. Squirrels' feet and claws are so efficient at climbing that they find no difficulty in scaling brick walls and tall garden fences. One of the funniest sights is youngsters playing and learning about their wonderful feet. Favourite exercises include suspending yourself upside down, and hanging from one leg before dropping in on an unsuspecting sibling, or racing round and round a tree-trunk rather like the legendary tiger that turned into butter.

Squirrel senses

Squirrels don't have any important natural predators in this country, so their senses are geared towards finding food and avoiding tree-climbing accidents. They have rounded faces, with large dark eyes capable of sharp all-round vision (with the exception of a small blind strip at the top of the field of view). Indeed, the density of light-sensitive cells on a squirrel's retina is exceptionally high compared to that of most other mammals. Researchers have found that squirrels see most colours as shades of grey, apart from yellow, which they can perceive. This is interesting, as to a red squirrel a grey probably looks grey, and to a grey squirrel, a red just looks dark grey. Squirrels are particularly sensitive to movement, and I have found that if you stay very still, wild squirrels will often come to within a few feet without actually noticing you (if they do take fright it is probably because they can smell you). However, a moving observer can be spotted several hundred yards away, and the squirrel will freeze in an attempt to hide.

Squirrels have large ears and sensitive hearing. They have a wide vocabulary of sounds which include a loud and piercing cry often used by youngsters in distress, and a whole series of chucks and chatters signalling alarm, threat and displeasure according to when and how they are used.

Smell is also an important squirrel sense. It is most likely that smell is used when selecting food items, and also to find buried hoards of nuts and seeds, called 'caches'. Squirrels mark patches of stripped bark with urine which can be smelled by strangers. These patches may be re-marked regularly suggesting that the animal is using its smell to signal its identity and presence to other squirrels. Since squirrels obviously cannot use colour variation as a method of recognizing one another, smell is probably the most likely way for them to tell individuals apart. Male squirrels respond to the smell of a female ready to mate, and both red and grey males have been recorded making very direct journeys of up to a kilometre from downwind of a female in breeding condition.

The squirrel's head is also covered with touch-sensitive whiskers, around the mouth, eyes and ears. These whiskers tell its front end that it is about to bump into something before it actually does, which is very useful if you are leaping about in the tree-tops in a force eight gale, and can't keep your eyes on quite everything. Whiskers are also found on the squirrel's feet, and at the base of its tail.

Fur and the moulting business

Both red and grey squirrels have very different summer and winter coats. The body fur is moulted twice a year, in spring and autumn, but the tail fur and ear-tufts of red squirrels are only moulted once, in the summer. A red squirrel in summer has a coarse, short coat of rich chestnut fur, which may have some grey fur around the flanks and head. The ear-tufts are very thin or absent altogether, the tail is thin, and the hairs of both are bleached to a creamy white. This may not be true in all cases, as interbreeding with introduced foreign sub-species has suppressed the characteristic ear- and tail-bleaching of some British red squirrels. Grey squirrels also have a short summer coat, of greyish brown banded hairs, with splashes of almost orange fur over the feet and along the ribs. The tail is very thin, and grey squirrels have no ear-tufts at all. Both squirrels have white bellies.

Any time between August and November, squirrels exchange their thin summer coats for heavier winter ones. The moult starts in the region of the rump and flanks, and progresses forwards towards the animal's head. The red squirrel grows a thick winter coat of long dark brown fur, although there is a great deal of variation in individual coat colours. The tail becomes a plume of dense, long fur, and the ear-tufts are very prominent. They are usually dark brown in colour, but will soon begin to bleach, so that they have reverted to a cream colour by about March. Grey squirrels have thick winter coats with a grizzled salt and pepper look to them. The individual hairs are banded with grey, yellowish brown, and tipped with white. The white tips are particularly obvious on the long tail fur. In reds and greys the belly remains white, and the naked palms of the feet may grow a thick covering of fur in winter. By about April, squirrels begin to moult into their summer coats again, and this time, the fur is first shed around the head, and the moult progresses backwards along the animal's body. On the Isle of Wight, I have seen a very late spring moult amongst red squirrels, which involved almost complete loss of the thick winter coat, leaving the squirrels to run about almost naked for four or five days before the summer coat had come through. Bald squirrels are really hideous.

Besides all shades of red and grey, squirrels of both species show some more drastic colour variations; black or melanistic red squirrels are very rare, but pale and even white ones, sometimes albinos, occur quite regularly. Black grey squirrels are much more common, particularly around the Woburn estate, and true albinos occur frequently in Kent, Surrey and Sussex. They are frequently seen in the grounds of my college, for example.

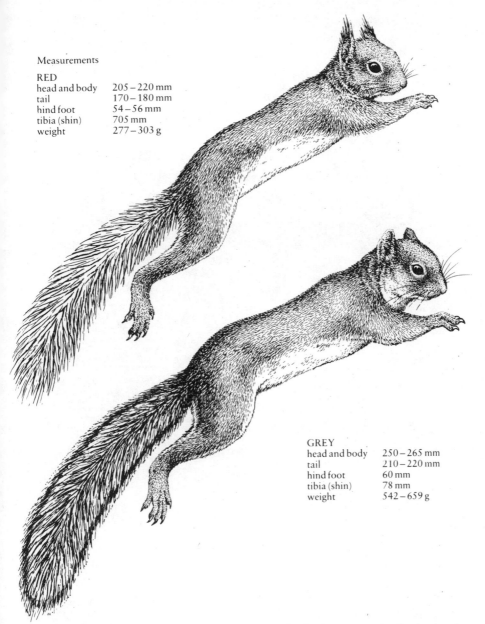

Measurements

RED

head and body	205 – 220 mm
tail	170 – 180 mm
hind foot	54 – 56 mm
tibia (shin)	705 mm
weight	277 – 303 g

GREY

head and body	250 – 265 mm
tail	210 – 220 mm
hind foot	60 mm
tibia (shin)	78 mm
weight	542 – 659 g

If you compare the bodies of red and grey squirrels, they are very similar in size, but rather different in shape. The grey squirrel is a heavy, stocky beast in comparison to its lighter and leggier cousin the red squirrel.

Three different commonly occurring red squirrel colour varieties, one pale buff, one very dark greyish brown, and one ginger.

Telling the sexes apart

If you persuade a squirrel to turn upside down for you and display its all, then the sexes are very easy to tell apart.

The female squirrel has a small anal opening, with a tiny fleshy protrusion (papilla) just in front of it, located very close to the tail. When the female is ready to mate, the vaginal opening is visible at the base of this papilla, but for much of the year, it is closed over and 'out of use'. The female also has four pairs of teats, which may be quite difficult to find in virgin females, but are more obvious in animals that have bred before. During lactation, these teats are very swollen, and often have large bald patches around them, where the fur has been rubbed away by suckling babies.

A male squirrel has a much larger gap between the papilla and the anus. The penis is quite obvious, just over a centimetre away from the anus and in the middle of the belly. When the male is young, that is probably all you can see. However, if he has been reproductively active before, the scrotum, between the penis and the anus, may well be stained darkly, or even black. Out of the breeding season the scrotum is empty, because the testes shrink and are withdrawn into the body cavity. When the male comes into reproductive condition, the testes descend into the scrotum, and begin to grow. I have always used a size score to tell how active a male is. When the

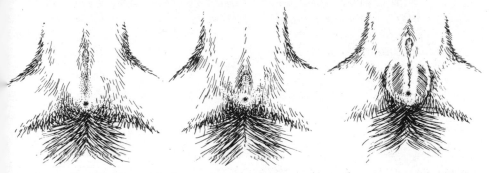

Male squirrel (left): *genital opening about 1 cm. from the anus; much smaller separation in female* (centre); *male in reproductive condition* (right).

testes are size one, they have just decended into the scrotum, and the male would not be capable of successful breeding. By the time they are size three, they are half grown, and the male is capable of mating. They do grow on to size five by the height of the season, and, to be honest, I sometimes wonder how male squirrels manage to climb trees in this condition.

The peculiar case of red grey squirrels and grey red squirrels

You might think that a red and a grey squirrel look completely different, but they are frequently confused, and at certain stages of their moult can be easily mixed up. Adult red squirrels in summer coat can grow a great deal of grey fur, and this, in conjunction with the bleached tail and thin ear-tufts, can make them look remarkably like grey squirrels. On the other hand, grey squirrels in summer coat can sometimes be almost completely covered with bright reddish yellow fur. You should be able to tell them apart by their shape and size. In summer coat red squirrels still retain their cute squirrel appearance, but with thin fur, the sparse tail and more rat-like features of the grey squirrel are accentuated. You could also be forgiven for mistaking a young grey squirrel for a red, as the patches of red fur on these youngsters are sometimes very vivid, and their smaller size makes them more likely candidates for confusion.

summer   winter

GREY

summer   winter

RED

Seasonal changes in the squirrel's coat.

From the inside

The soft bits of a squirrel's insides are pretty ordinary. As a typical rodent, it has quite a large stomach, and long intestines designed to absorb as much as possible from a bulky vegetarian diet. Squirrels lay down fat under the skin and around major organs in preparation for the winter. The fat insulates the animal, and can provide a valuable energy store in the case of severe food shortage. It is notable that grey squirrels seem better equipped for fat storage, gaining about 25% body weight before the winter to the red's meagre 12%. This could have serious implications in the event of a hard winter, the grey squirrel having a better survival kit against starvation.

The skeleton

The squirrel's skeleton is specialized for climbing and leaping. Features to note are a strong spine, extended down the back into a very long tail, which is used mainly as a balance organ. Both the hips and the shoulders are well developed for support and attachment of muscles which work the limbs. If you take measurements from the skeletons of red and grey squirrels, you get quite a surprise. Placing one of each side by side, there is only a couple of inches difference in the lengths of the two animals nose to tail. There is even less of a difference between the lengths of their hind limbs. This is

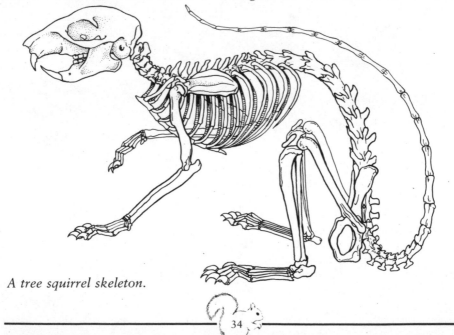

A tree squirrel skeleton.

interesting, because you will remember that grey squirrels weigh nearly twice as much as reds. This suggests a substantial difference in the proportions of the two animals. Red squirrels are thin and leggy, which makes them very agile and well suited to leaping about in trees. Grey squirrels on the other hand are quite heavy for their size, much stockier, and probably a good deal less agile. As you will see later, these differences in body proportions are reflected in squirrel behaviour. Reds seem to spend much more time feeding aloft, where their agile frame serves them well whilst greys prefer to spend more time on the ground.

There is quite a considerable difference in the skulls of red and grey squirrels. The length of the skull from the back of the head to the tip of the nose is usually over 1.2 cm. (half an inch) longer on the grey, and the most marked difference in the animals' appearance is that red squirrels have shorter, more rounded noses. Both squirrels have quite flat heads with wide, strong cheek-bones.

The jaws and teeth
Basically, squirrels go through life with a very efficient pair of nutcrackers attached to the front of their faces. The first of a baby squirrel's teeth to erupt are the incisors, two upper and two lower, which break through at about three weeks of age. Then come the cheek teeth, three upper and three lower molars with strong grinding ridges on the surface, and two upper and

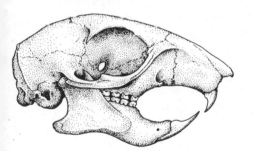 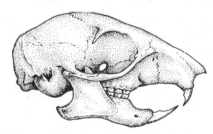

Comparison of skulls of a grey (left) and a red (right) squirrel.

one lower pre-molars. The lower and second upper pre-molars will be shed at about 16 weeks, and replaced with adult teeth, the rest are permanent. There are no canine teeth, which is common amongst herbivores and the gap that they leave is called the diastema. This is very useful, as the squirrel can draw its cheeks into the gap, separating its mouth into two chambers, one for biting and one for chewing. In other rodents, this system is further developed to provide food-storing pouches at the front. It's also very useful if you want to feed a sick, reluctant squirrel which won't open its mouth (see p.70).

The most specialized of the squirrel's teeth are the incisors at the front. These teeth have yellow coloured enamel on only the front surface, meaning that the softer dentine tissues wear from behind to a very sharp cutting edge. Squirrels' teeth wear quickly (the incisors at up to a couple of millimetres per week), but, in common with all other rodents, they have developed a way of dealing with this problem. The teeth of most mammals stop growing soon after eruption, when the blood supply is cut as the soft centre of the tooth, the pulp cavity, seals off. Rodent incisors have a very large pulp cavity with an excellent blood supply which stays open throughout the animal's life. This means that as the teeth wear at the tip, they are continually being replaced by new growth from the base.

A system of continual tooth growth is fine, so long as your upper and lower teeth meet in the middle to grind against each other evenly. The incisors are the front line of attack on a tough diet, and if upper and lower

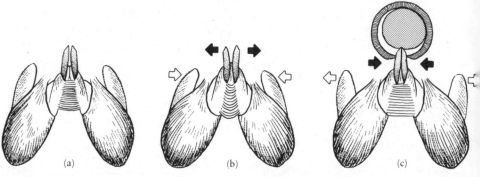

(a) (b) (c)

The squirrel's nutcrackers. At rest (a) the incisor teeth point straight upwards to oppose their counterparts in the upper jaw. Opened (b) the incisors are prepared for seizing a food item, and finally (c) closed together for chiselling into and prizing open nuts. Armed with perfect gnawing teeth, the squirrel's jaws are further specialized for the task of cracking nuts. The lower jaw is in two halves, joined by the trans-versus mandibular muscle which can pull them together. Two other muscles, the deep and the superficial masseters, can act to stretch the trans-versus mandibular, and thus pull the two halves of the lower jaw apart slightly. At rest, the lower incisors point straight upwards, but with the trans-versus mandibular contracted, they point out into an open 'V' for seizing food. When the trans-versus mandibular is stretched by the other two muscles, the incisors are pulled together at their tips, making a strong chisel edge for prizing nuts open.

teeth do not oppose each other accurately, the squirrel is in trouble. The incisors will continue to grow in a spiral, unchecked by wear, and whereas those in the lower jaw will just grow into huge tusks which may well get broken off, the upper incisors can grow right round in an arc to pierce first the throat, and eventually the skull, resulting in the squirrel's demise. Fortunately, this is very infrequent.

Do squirrels bite?

Yes! A squirrel can inflict a very nasty bite, usually made worse by the automatic reaction of the victim to draw away, thus tearing the flesh. I have never been bitten by a grey squirrel, mostly because I always wear thick leather falconry gauntlets whilst handling them. However, I only use gardening gloves for handling reds, as they are considerably smaller, and it is difficult to find the correct grip through a thick pair of gloves. Consequently I have been bitten many times by reds, and have the scars to prove it. Somehow they always choose to do it when you have an audience and cannot let forth the torrent of expletives *demanded by the occasion. I heard a lovely story from the woodman at one of my study sites. He told of a red squirrel collecting expedition he'd made when he was a boy. He and a friend set off to catch baby squirrels with the aid of a big stick with which to hit the drey tree, and a sack for their prizes. One squirrel proved a bit reluctant to comply, and, having fallen from its tree, it ran round and round in circles and eluded capture. Suddenly it was gone, but its whereabouts were given away by the expression of anguish on one boy's face as the squirrel shot up his trousers and sank its teeth firmly into his behind. Serves him right!*

How long do squirrels live . . . and what kills them?

For a squirrel it seems that it all depends whether you make it to your first birthday. The dangers start as soon as the squirrel is born. Its mother may not manage to produce enough milk, and the baby may starve in the litter drey. In my experience of both red and grey squirrels, such failed litters are not very common, and when they do occur, tend to be the result of exceptional conditions. For the most part, if a female squirrel does breed at all, the young will reach weaning age.

This is when things start to get tough, and by far the highest proportion of deaths in a squirrel population is accounted for by youngsters under one year of age. These young squirrels are very inexperienced, and the most common cause of death is starvation, particularly during a bad British summer. This would be a time of year when supplementary feeding of red squirrels could boost the survival of young enormously, and prevent a

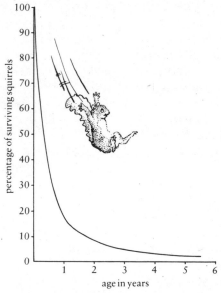

The squirrel's chances of survival.

population crash if the ensuing winter was a bad one. Once a squirrel has made it past the age of one, be it red or grey, it is not uncommon for it to live on to four or even five years of age in the wild, longer in captivity.

Even in the case of adult squirrels, starvation is still the number one killer. Squirrels have no serious natural predators in Britain now, although they may fall prey to domestic cats and dogs. I lost a red squirrel at one of my study sites to an escaped goshawk, another was run over by a rampant steam train, and a radio-tagged grey squirrel I was once tracking managed to get itself ploughed. Cars are a big danger to squirrels, and many are killed on the roads. Males in the spring time (when they have their minds on the fairer sex, and not the highway code) seem particularly vulnerable, as do younger, less streetwise squirrels. In both cases, the squirrels are probably travelling about more than usual (the males to find a mate, and the youngsters to find somewhere to settle down), increasing the likelihood of having to cross a road, and losing a fight with a car.

Squirrels do succumb to various diseases, the most important being Coccidiosis and parapoxvirus (sse p.19). Coccidiosis is a type of enteritis caused by a gut parasite called *Eimeria sciurorum*. It is very unpleasant, and the squirrel will normally become wasted and suffer from very severe diarrhoea before dying. This disease affects both red and grey squirrels. Parapoxvirus has so far only been recorded amongst red squirrels, and has been mistaken for myxomatosis. The virus lodges in the squirrel's eyelids,

and they become very puffed and swollen, often running with discharge as well. As with rabbit myxomatosis, the disease is very debilitating, and is highly contagious. Unable to see, and apparently very lethargic, infected squirrels stagger about and soon die, as they are completely unable to function normally. If you find a squirrel suffering from a bad dose of either of these diseases, probably the kindest thing that you could do is to put the animal out of its misery. However, it would also be a good idea to report the incident to the Ministry of Agriculture Veterinary Investigation Centre (address supplied at back of book), as they may well be interested in doing a post mortem to improve our knowledge of these diseases. The same is true of red squirrels that have been killed on the road, since healthy bodies can also be useful in research.

There are a number of other nasties that squirrels carry around with them. One is the fungus *Microsporum cookei* which causes a ringworm infection characterized by crusty and flaking ears. This does not appear to bother the squirrel unduly, but I have been informed by a veterinary surgeon that although rare, it can be very unpleasant if passed on to dogs. None of these diseases is harmful to humans.

How to tell a squirrel's age

Telling the age of a squirrel is really very difficult. For the purposes of most field studies, members of a population will simply be assigned age 'classes'. This is the equivalent of saying that a child is a 'toddler' or a 'teenager' rather than giving it an accurate age. Very young squirrels are distinctive because of their light weight, small structure, and an overall 'stringy' appearance, with a thin tail and no signs of sexual maturity. Adults are generally heavier, larger, with thicker, bushy tails, and for most of the year some signs of sexual maturity, either testes decended into the scrotum, or

swollen nipples in the female (see p.31). The 'inbetweenies' can be quite difficult to sort out, particularly amongst red squirrels.

It sometimes helps to take body measurements, especially when tackling these adolescent animals. Weight is an obvious test, although there is an enormous amount of individual and seasonal variation to take into account. Better to record weight in conjunction with some other body measurement to make sure. This prevents mix-ups like being tempted to call a heavy animal an adult without realizing that it is in fact quite small, and just a well fed youngster. Conversely a light animal might be mistaken for a yearling, until you realize that it is actually a fully grown but skinny adult. It is impossible to persuade a wild squirrel to lie on a ruler so that you can measure its head and body length, so I always use shin length, as this can be measured using a pair of calipers, with the animal immobilized in a handling cone (see p.107).

Age determination of dead squirrels can be more accurate. For a start, you can take much more complete measurements than you can from one that's alive and wriggling about. Squirrel teeth are very useful in ageing. It is obviously no good using the incisors, as they grow continually and would not give much of a clue to the age of your subject. However, the degree of wear on its cheek teeth can be of much more help. If the body is very fresh, you can be really macabre and remove its eye lenses. These increase in weight as the animal gets older, and thus a simple measurement of their weight can give you a fairly accurate estimate of age, to the nearest year. For young animals, you could also look at the skeleton for clues. Squirrel bones continue to grow until the animal is mature at between a year and eighteen months old. They grow from special soft areas called 'epiphyses' which slowly turn to hard bone as the animal reaches its full size. These soft areas are very obvious in the long bones of the legs and arms, at the ankles and wrists. X-rays will show the degree of hardening or closure of the epiphyses, and this can give a good estimate of a young animal's age. The method works with other mammals too, including us.

Squirrel parasites

Your image of this cuddly and irreproachable creature would be shattered if you got a really close look at the bunch of undesirables that squirrels carry around with them. For starters, they are invariably hopping with fleas. In the case of the red squirrel, *Monopsyllus sciurorum* is the guilty party, and of the grey *Orchopeas howardii* (which occasionally hops onto the red squirrel). Squirrels get their fleas from their mother whilst still in the nest. The parasites actually spend quite a bit of their time just sitting about in the squirrel's nest lining, hopping on for a meal when the animal comes home to rest. However, every time I handle a squirrel, I am reminded that they also tote around a large number of the little beggars in their fur. These will readily jump onto humans, but I have never been bitten by one.

Squirrel fleas can be transferred to your dog. However, dogs don't very often come into contact with squirrels, and of all the fleas that the average dog carries, less than 2 per cent originally came from a squirrel. Wild mammals are frequently blamed for transferring fleas to pet dogs and cats, but further investigation has shown that wild mammals fade into insignificance when placed alongside the domestic cat as a donor of fleas. Remove all of your dog's little friends, and you will find that over 80 per cent of them were given to him by cats, some 12 per cent are dog fleas, and of the remaining 8 per cent, the largest proportion was collected from household

pests like mice and rats. As you can see, it really is unfair to blame wild mammals for your problems.

Squirrels also carry ticks, mites and lice, but these rarely cause the animal any trouble, and are often not present at all.

Do pine martens eat squirrels?

If there were to be a significant natural predator of squirrels in this country, the pine marten would be the most likely candidate. Indeed, they are often singled out as important red squirrel predators in the literature. This, however, is not the case in the British Isles, although red squirrels do form a major part of *the diet of Swedish and Finnish pine martens.*

The present distribution of pine martens in Britain is very restricted, and they are now only to be found in central and northern Scotland, dotted about northern England, a very few places in Wales, and on the east and western coasts of Ireland.

Pine martin.

Studies have shown that they have a varied diet, which rarely includes squirrel. Other smaller rodents are an important food, and pine martens seem to show a preference for field voles (Microtus agrestis). Small birds, particularly wrens, tits and tree creepers are taken, mostly roosting individuals. Other food items include beetles, caterpillars, bird's eggs, fish, berries and even carrion. In season, pine martens eat a lot of wild raspberries, and why not? It's a lot easier than chasing squirrels about, and berries aren't likely to put up much of a fight.

Where do squirrels live?

Slightly eccentric squirrels have been found running about in fields, on motorways miles from anywhere and living in rabbit holes out in the open, but for the average squirrel, woodland is home. Woods are good places to live. They are relatively sheltered and warm. They provide a totally three-dimensional environment, meaning that the squirrel can exploit up and down, as well as side to side. Woods are naturally a relatively undisturbed and stable habitat, although modern forestry practices mean that squirrels frequently have to be good at moving house quickly.

What makes a wood good for squirrels? In short, plenty of food, shelter, and other squirrels. Best of all are old woods, where a system of natural regeneration or coppice provides a constant flush of new growth beneath the mature seed-bearing trees. This thick understorey gives good ground cover, and, in the case of hazel coppice, can be an extremely important food source for both species of squirrel. A mixture of tree species is always best, since if the seed crop of one species fails in a particular year, there will always be others to feed upon.

Well established and managed woods make the best habitat, as not only are the trees of better quality, but all the other associated plants have had time to develop. The food source that they provide can be very important in the event of a shortage of tree seed, for example bulbs, fungi and berries (see p.74). Squirrels can be found living in younger woods; some conifers begin to bear cones after only 25 years, and young beech and sycamore are regularly ravaged by squirrels feeding on their sweet sap.

Important native tree species for squirrels include oak, beech, hazel, ash, field maple, hornbeam, Scots pine and even yew. Amongst the introduced species squirrels make good use of sweet chestnut, sycamore, various types of spruce and larch as well as Douglas fir. The berries of shrubs like hawthorn and blackthorn provide good seasonal food, as do the fruit of alder and crab apple. I am sure that more could be added to this list, which just highlights the opportunistic nature of these beasts.

Squirrels regularly travel down corridors between woods, either over-grown hedgerows, or fringes of woodland planted as shelter belts for farms, crops or houses. Grey squirrels tend to take to the open far more readily than reds, and are commonly found in urban parks and gardens. Red squirrels certainly frequent these haunts in Europe and used to in this country, but they are very rarely seen in cities and towns in Britain today.

Home sweet home

The squirrel's nest is a very important place – after all, the animal spends a great deal of time there. Tree squirrels do not hibernate, and thus during the cold winter months the nest must provide sufficient protection against the cold to allow the occupant to rest and sleep without freezing or getting wet. For the squirrel it's a bit like crawling into an extra thick, energy saving overcoat. A nest used in winter must therefore, be robust, water- and windproof, and also warm. During the summer months, the squirrel's nest must provide a convenient place for resting during the activity of long days (although squirrels frequently snooze on exposed branches during long periods of summer foraging), as well as at night and it must also be a safe place for rearing young.

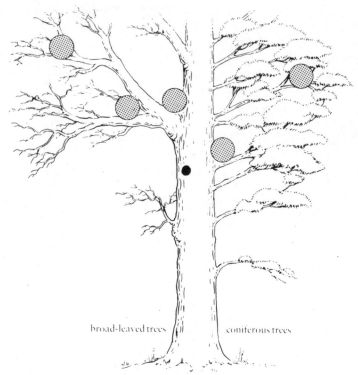

broad-leaved trees   coniferous trees

Where to look for squirrel dreys and dens.

There are two types of squirrel nest. Dreys are the characteristic domed nests that you find in trees and may confuse with those of birds like magpies and crows (see p.55). Dens are carefully lined tree hollows, often made in the vacated homes of hole-nesting birds like woodpeckers. Although dreys are usually the most common type of squirrel nest, the proportion of dens and dreys is largely dependent upon the availability of suitable nesting sites. For example, there are few hollow trees or woodpecker holes in young plantations.

Squirrels seem to prefer to build their nests high up in trees, at a height of 6m. (18 ft.) or more (although there is a great deal of individual variation,

sticks leaves

grass moss

A cross-section view of a squirrel winter drey.

and the nest-building squirrel obviously has to make do with a short tree if that is all that is available). Whilst dreys are big and conspicuous, particularly after the autumn leaf fall, dens are very difficult to find, since all that is visible is the entrance hole. Really the only way to be sure that a tree hollow is being used by a squirrel is actually to see the animal entering or leaving. There are other signs, like claw marks on the trunk around the entrance hole, and teeth marks on its inner surface, indicating squirrel occupation, but you will often need a long ladder to find them and experience to tell the work of a squirrel from that of other animals.

Dreys are easier to find, as they are built in the open, supported by the tree-trunk or branches, or in creepers hanging from them. In coniferous trees, dreys are most frequently built close to the straight trunk, and out of the prevailing wind. In branching species like the Monterey pine (*Pinus radiata*) or yew (*Taxus baccata*), dreys may be built in the crown under the protection of the thick canopy. In deciduous trees, dreys are built in trunk or branch forks where they will be protected from the elements after the leaves have fallen, or in amongst trailing creepers like ivy or honeysuckle, and less often amongst the exposed twigs of the crown. I have often read that you can tell the difference between red and grey squirrel dreys because red squirrels always build nests in conifers and greys in deciduous trees. However, in my experience, this simply isn't the case, and I have records of the dreys of both species being built in both types of tree.

Young squirrels do not usually make the world's best architects.

Suitable trees are most probably selected for their shelter value. There is no doubt that a drey will afford its occupant much better protection from the elements when sited beneath a thick evergreen canopy, or tucked away in the fork between two sturdy branches, rather than built in an open leafless crown to be lashed by the winter winds and rain. It is likely that there is a certain degree of learning involved in prudent drey positioning. In studies of both red and grey squirrels, nursing females tend to move out of the sturdy litter drey at weaning, and into one of their other dreys, leaving it to the young. As the youngsters disperse from their litter drey, they may use the dreys of other adults in the vicinity before building the first of their own. Whilst watching tagged red squirrels beginning to fend for themselves after about twelve weeks of age, I have seen some very miserable early drey-building efforts, often abandoned as a bad lot after a single, obviously uncomfortable night. These dreys tended to be loosely woven, and often sited in tree crowns or the forks of young trees. In bad weather, youngsters may even succumb to exposure sleeping in such poorly constructed nests, so it pays to either hijack somebody else's nest, or learn fast how to build a good'un.

Building a nest

It is no haphazard business to build a good nest, and squirrels take a great deal of time and trouble in the construction of a drey or den. This is reflected in the fact that, with minor refurbishments, most nests last for at least two seasons, and some for considerably longer.

Drey-building usually commences with the construction of a platform of woven twigs, although the squirrel may cheat and use the base of an old drey or a bird's nest as its starting point. The domed top is then constructed by interlacing twigs and leaves, the squirrel becoming increasingly choosey about nest material as the structure nears completion. Although many of the twigs used for building are selected and cut from the tree in which the squirrel works, frequently journeys of many metres are made through the treetops for just the right twig, sprig of leaves or piece of bark. There is some difference in the nest materials chosen by red and grey squirrels for this part of the job. Grey squirrels will use twigs covered in fresh leaves more often than reds, who tend to strip leaves off the twigs of deciduous trees, but will leave needles on conifer twigs. Red squirrels are more likely to pack out the superstructure of bare twigs with dead leaves, moss and bark. In both cases, construction starts with larger twigs, often longer than 10–15 cm. (4 or 5 inches), the size getting gradually finer as the structure progresses.

Most of the work is done using the front feet, nose and mouth, and every so often the squirrel will dive inside the developing nest to keep it hollow and try it out for size. Some dreys are built with an entrance, but it is just as common for the squirrel to simply force its way into the nest through the thick wall of twigs. Once the squirrel is satisfied with the superstructure of the drey, the task of gathering lining material begins. This can take a considerable time, as the animal makes repeated journeys to collect moss, thistledown, dried grass and feathers – anything soft. Some squirrels go completely overboard with the interior decoration of their homes, and I have examined dreys lined with sheep's wool, shredded paper hankies, and one very tasteful one was lined with an entire ball of pale yellow baby wool.

The finished red squirrel drey is about 30cm. (12 inches) across, but that of the grey may be quite a bit bigger. It has probably taken at least a day to build, and I have recorded squirrels returning to the job for as long as five days. The twig and leaf walls are about 5–7cm. (2–3 inches) thick for nests used in winter, with a luxurious lining of soft bedding material. In summer dreys may be entirely constructed of much lighter materials, like honeysuckle bast (stripped bark), but you are unlikely to find these, as they are

easily hidden, and nowhere near as long-lasting as the more robust winter dreys.

Dens do not require as much work on the part of the squirrel. The entrance made by a woodpecker may need a bit of enlargement and any draughty bits inside the hollow will be blocked up with twigs and leaves, but apart from this, it's just a question of lining the nest. Having said that, I once inspected a den which had belonged to one of my study animals, since deceased. The den had a long narrow entrance just big enough to get your hand into, and the hollow inside was quite large. The squirrel had filled the den with the best part of a sackful of moss which must have taken days to collect. Needless to say, I left it all intact for another squirrel to use – no point in wasting all that effort.

How many nests?

Squirrels usually have more than one nest in use at any time, swapping between dreys or dens every few days. This behaviour has several obvious advantages. Firstly, should your nest get wet, or even be destroyed in bad weather, you always have another in reserve. This is particularly important for nursing females. Secondly, squirrels carry a lot of external parasites. Fleas are a particular problem. Some of these parasites travel around with the squirrel, but the majority remain in amongst the nest lining material, and just hop on for a meal when the squirrel is at home. Indeed, the best way to test whether a nest is currently in use is to place your hand inside for a few seconds (preferably when the squirrel is out if you wish to avoid injury), withdraw it and look for fleas. The parasites respond to the heat of your hand, mistaking it for the returning squirrel, and leap on for food. I have never been bitten by a squirrel flea, but they are very irritating as they scuttle about under your clothing. By changing dreys at regular intervals, the squirrel may reduce the level of parasite infestation by leaving the fleas behind and unfed every so often. Of course, by using one another's dreys, squirrels also share one another's fleas.

People often ask if it is possible to estimate the number of squirrels living in their local wood by counting nests. I am afraid that this is a bit tricky. Apart from the fact that it is virtually impossible to include dens in such a count since they are so difficult to see, both red and grey squirrels use more than one drey at a time. It is also common for the remains of old dreys, not to mention crow or magpie nests to linger on for a long time, and from down on the ground it is easy to mistake them for occupied dreys, especially in pine trees, or in the summer when everything is hidden by leaves. Basically, the presence of dreys should be used as an indication that squirrels are around, but the number of them does not exactly reflect population size, not least because they all use each others'.

Nest sharing

Nest sharing amongst squirrels is very common, although they usually only share with other local squirrels, rather than those from farther afield. I have seen an unwelcome lodger (dropping in for a rest whilst on a long-distance foray) expelled with violent force by a female red squirrel who then allowed a neighbour to snuggle up in her drey about ten minutes later. There seems to be no apparent selection of a drey mate on grounds of age or sex, but it does seem to be important that the squirrels 'know' each other (see p.100). Sharing does not just stop at two squirrels either. There are records of four red squirrels sleeping together, and as many as seven greys stuffed into one bulging drey – either having a party or a prayer meeting? I've been told of the discovery of a den containing some nine dead grey squirrels. It seems that the last one in had turned round and blocked the entrance, hence the air supply, thus imprisoning its bedmates and causing their deaths by suffocation. These pile-ups most commonly occur in the colder months, and the motto seems to be, why get cold when you can share with a friend?

The more adventurous home-builder

Most squirrels are conventional, and build their nests in trees, but reports abound of more bizarre sites chosen by the more radical of our little furry friends. Red squirrels have been discovered nesting in hollow fallen trees, holes in the ground and in low bushes, whilst their grey cousins have been known to nest in rabbit holes, bilberry bushes (*Vaccinium*) and in amongst tree roots. Squirrels don't mind sharing a roof with us, either. They will happily build dens in amongst roofing thatch, under tiles and in grant-aided roof insulation. Squirrels are frequent residents of church towers, and have even been known to nest in cavity walls. Urban greys are particularly good

Grey squirrel carrying nest material to line its new residence, built beneath the tiles of somebody's roof.

at finding original places to live. They do not just visit your bird table, but may chew their way into the local bird box . . . a bit of a squeeze, but less effort than building one yourself. The smaller red squirrel finds it especially easy to make use of tit boxes, and I have recently heard of a place in Scotland where starlings under study were regularly evicted from their nest boxes by house-hunting red squirrels.

Squirrel drey or magpie's nest?

It is really quite difficult to tell the difference between a large bird's nest and a squirrel drey from the ground. There are several clues, though. Birds are much more likely to build in the crown of a tree, whereas squirrels tuck their dreys into clefts out of the wind. Magpies in particular prefer tall bushes like

hawthorn, whilst squirrels rarely build dreys below 5 m. (15 feet) high in a tree. Also, you may be able to see light through the loosely interlaced twigs of a bird's nest or a disused drey, whereas a squirrel drey in use is very dense and compactly built. Thirdly, birds usually perch around their nests,

and may leave tell-tale white droppings either on surrounding branches, or on the ground at the base of the nest tree. The only way to be really sure is to get a close look at the structure — then the answer will become obvious because the bird's nest has a flat top, whilst the squirrel's drey has a domed roof. Furthermore, magpies (and other birds that build nests big enough to be confused with dreys) tend to use dead twigs for their nests, whilst squirrels, particularly greys, like to use fresh twigs, often with leaves still attached.

Telling red from grey squirrel dreys is equally difficult, because, as we have seen, they use the same methods of construction, similar or identical nest materials, and build in similar trees. Grey squirrel dreys are usually a bit bigger than reds, but size is very difficult to assess from the ground. A good clue is the density of dreys. Squirrel population density will be discussed in more detail later in the text, but suffice it to say for now that in a wood of a given size, you would expect to find at least two or three times as many grey squirrels as you would reds. Thus, if there are lots of dreys visible in a wood, it is probably occupied by greys rather than reds. Indeed, in my experience it is quite difficult to see red squirrel dreys, but in a wood occupied by grey squirrels, virtually every large tree seems to have one.

Mating

Red and grey squirrels have very similar breeding biology, but they do not interbreed. Despite there being equal numbers of males and females in the population, squirrels do not form stable pairs, and males may mate with more than one female during the breeding season. Female squirrels are not very liberated, and the male takes no part at all in the raising of offspring; that job is left to her alone.

Both male and female squirrels become sexually mature at about eleven months of age, but that doesn't necessarily mean that they will begin to breed. Squirrel breeding is strongly influenced by the availability of a good food supply, and if the animals are hungry and in poor condition they will not be inclined to breed. Assuming that all is well, a healthy male squirrel will be ready to mate at just about any time of the year, although some do take a few months off between September and November. Females have two seasons of oestrus cycles each year, and, if they are in good condition, can produce two litters with an average of three youngsters in each. Pregnancy lasts for 38 days for red squirrels and 44 days for greys, and although litters can be produced at almost any time of year (except perhaps mid-winter), they are normally concentrated into two periods, the first during spring in March and April, and the second later on in the summer during June and July, but young may be born in the south of England as early as January, and as late as September.

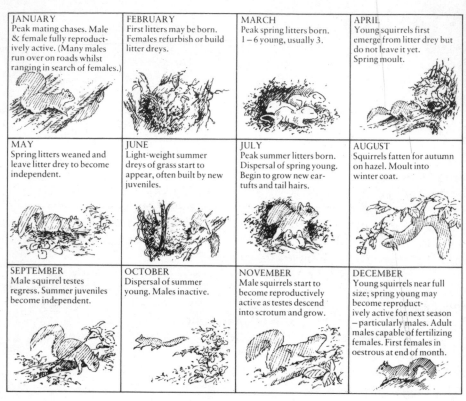

JANUARY Peak mating chases. Male & female fully reproductively active. (Many males run over on roads whilst ranging in search of females.)	**FEBRUARY** First litters may be born. Females refurbish or build litter dreys.	**MARCH** Peak spring litters born. 1 – 6 young, usually 3.	**APRIL** Young squirrels first emerge from litter drey but do not leave it yet. Spring moult.
MAY Spring litters weaned and leave litter drey to become independent.	**JUNE** Light-weight summer dreys of grass start to appear, often built by new juveniles.	**JULY** Peak summer litters born. Dispersal of spring young. Begin to grow new ear-tufts and tail hairs.	**AUGUST** Squirrels fatten for autumn on hazel. Moult into winter coat.
SEPTEMBER Male squirrel testes regress. Summer juveniles become independent.	**OCTOBER** Dispersal of summer young. Males inactive.	**NOVEMBER** Male squirrels start to become reproductively active as testes descend into scrotum and grow.	**DECEMBER** Young squirrels near full size; spring young may become reproductively active for next season – particularly males. Adult males capable of fertilizing females. First females in oestrous at end of month.

The squirrel's year.

Squirrel courtship is a noisy business, and the best time to look out for this behaviour is during the months of January and February. Of course, courtship does occur at other times of the year, particularly in April and May before the summer breeding season, but it is much more difficult to spot squirrels once there are leaves on the trees. A female ready to mate most probably smells good, because it is notable that most of her suitors will arrive from downwind. The first male on the scene (1) will start his suit by following the female (2) very closely, continually trying to attract her attention by flicking his tail, slapping bark with his front paws, and chattering loudly. It may well be all of this commotion which helps the late arrivals to home in on the action. The attentive male continues to try and get close to the object of his desire, until it all gets a bit much for her, and the mating chase begins. She makes a dash for it, and, hotly pursued by her

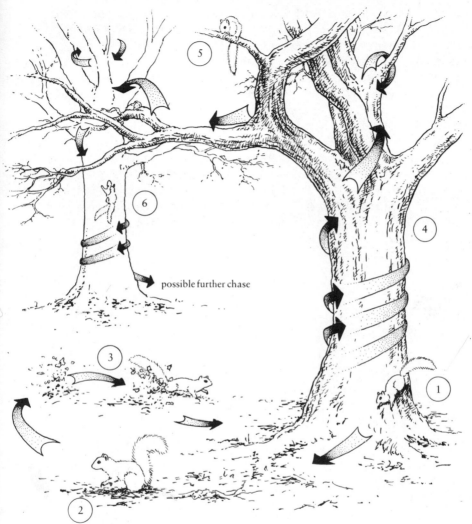

possible further chase

The goings on of a squirrel courtship or mating chase.

suitor (3), the pair race through the tree-tops, up, down and around trunks (4), every-which-way; all this is accompanied by wild chattering and excitement. During the activity, the other males (5) just sit about watching, until one eventually plucks up the courage to join in and challenge. The whole palaver is repeated . . . and repeated, until the female finally allows one of the males to mate with her (6). She will normally signal her readiness to mate by chattering softly to the male (probably too exhausted to do anything by that stage), and allowing him to approach her side on with his tail stretched forwards along his body. All the matings that I have seen have taken place with the female clinging to the bark of a tree trunk facing upwards. The male approaches her from behind and mounts, clasping her around the tummy. She will flick her tail out to one side, allowing him to mate successfully, and as soon as he has, they part and begin an intensive grooming session. I once watched a two-day mating chase between a female red squirrel and three males. The female didn't allow any of the males to mate with her at the end of the first day, and retired to her drey early. The three males, their rivalry obviously dampened by sheer exhaustion, slept together in a nearby drey, and the whole frenzy started up again bright and early the next morning. Females may mate several times during the chase, but thereafter will generally rebuff any further advances.

Raising a family

During her pregnancy, the female will prepare the nest in which she will raise her young. This may involve refurbishment of an existing den or drey, or construction of a new one, but it is usually a bit more luxurious than the run-of-the-mill home. The young are born blind, deaf, naked and completely helpless. The normal number in a litter is three babies, but there may be any number between one and six. During the first week the female visits them frequently, and, when she does have to feed, she doesn't travel more than 100 yards or so from the nest. As the young get older, she leaves them for longer periods and travels further afield. She has four pairs of nipples (more nipples than babies), which are very hard to see at the start of lactation, but once the young have been tugging at her for a few weeks, they become enlarged and all the fur around them gets worn away.

Female squirrels suckle their young for about 8 to 10 weeks.

By the time the babies are three weeks old, they have a fuzz of fur all over, and shortly afterwards their eyes and ears open. At this early age, their claws are surprisingly well developed, and they can support their own weight whilst clinging to tree bark, or an observer's jumper. At about this time, the young squirrel's teeth begin to appear, and they will start to chew at bits of bark or twig inside the nest. The female now begins to leave her

If a female squirrel is disturbed whilst she has young in the nest, she may well move them one by one to a safer place.

young for longer periods, to feed. Lactation puts a great strain on her, but studies suggest that few young die in the nest, probably because females just won't breed unless they are fit enough.

Female squirrels are very protective of their babies, and will chase away any other squirrel that might dare to approach too close to the nest tree. Should the litter drey be disturbed in any way, she will move her young to a safer place. Even well grown babies will be carefully carried, one by one to a new nest, sometimes over considerable distances. A radio-tagged female grey squirrel once moved her young three times during their infancy, ending up at the nest they'd started in. Perhaps the decor just wasn't quite to her taste.

At about seven weeks of age, the young squirrels look like miniature versions of their parents, and they are beginning to venture out of the nest for the first time. Following close on mother's heels, the youngsters soon gain confidence, and can be seen playing for hours in and around the nest

(Right) *Playful youngsters exploring outside their litter drey.*

tree. At this stage, they are still suckling, but they have started to try solid foods. By ten weeks of age, Mum is taking longer leaves of absence, and may not return to the nest every night. She hardly suckles the young at all, and they have begun to fend for themselves. They will soon learn to find food, and seem to spend a great deal of time obsessively burying what they find. It is common for siblings to stay close to one another at first, but any time between ten and fourteen weeks of age, they will move out into a new nest and begin to live alone.

These first few weeks are very important, particularly for young squirrels born in the summer. They are growing fast and must feed well in order to gain sufficient weight before the winter comes. An undernourished baby is far more likely to starve as the weather gets colder, as it will simply not have the energy to keep warm whilst out and about.

Young squirrels about 5 weeks old.

Caring for orphaned baby squirrels

You have to be very careful about looking after wild squirrels. You will need a licence to keep a red squirrel because it is a legally protected member of our British mammal fauna (see p.123), and you will need a different licence for a grey, because it is officially classed as vermin; animals which you may keep, but which you must not release. So contact your nearest Nature Conservancy Council office for legal advice or NCC Headquarters, see p. 125.

Alas, baby squirrels are frequently made homeless when the breeding nest of a female is destroyed during woodland management procedures. You cannot blame the woodman, he has to do his job. I have met many who will always avoid trees with red squirrel dreys in them, but it is impossible to know if there is a den in a hollow branch, and if you avoided all the trees with grey squirrel dreys in them, there wouldn't be anything left to cut down. It is rare for the unfortunate babies to be collected, mostly because if they can escape, they will, and it is only very tiny youngsters who have not yet opened their eyes that remain helpless as their nest plummets groundwards. Providing that they don't die of the initial shock, or from the cold, rescued baby squirrels are quite straightforward to look after, so long as you remember the golden rule of keeping the babies in a very constant environment, at an even temperature and with regular food and clean bedding.

Above all, they need warmth; not to be roasted, just kept warm. A small cardboard box makes a good substitute drey. Fill the box with hay, and make a nest hollow in the middle which you can line with shredded tissue paper, old socks or anything soft and warm. Put a hot-water bottle inside a thick sack and place it under the hay, or keep the box near the boiler or Rayburn, but do make sure that the temperature stays constant. Do not leave the babies exposed to draughts or damp, and give them plenty of clean, soft bedding to nuzzle into. If their eyes are not open yet, then you will find them easy to look after, and they will think that you are Mum when they do begin to see, and become quickly tame. If their eyes are already open, they may be a little more difficult to feed at first, but they will settle down. I managed to pull a litter of tailless greys through once; the chainsaw had clipped a little too close to their drey, but they settled quickly, and grew up to look rather peculiar.

For feeding the youngsters you can use any of the powdered milks sold for young animals, like puppy milk or lamb's milk, but, whatever you do, once you've started with one sort, stick to it. If you are lucky, you can get hold of a special small animal feeding bottle from some suppliers; but if not, a pipette or small syringe (without the needle) from your local vet will do. The youngsters will need feeding every two hours at first and they probably won't take very much at each feed, but as they settle down and develop a better appetite, you can reduce the number of feeds gradually. Once their eyes are open, at about three weeks, they should be fed every four hours, and given as much milk as they will take. If you feed them last thing at night, say 11 p.m., they will last through until 6 a.m. so long as they are warm. As their teeth begin to erupt, you can offer them things to chew. Small pieces of bark, dog biscuits or straw will do. Gradually reduce the number of feeds a day, until you begin to wean the baby squirrels at about eight weeks of age, by which time they will be quite a handful.

During and after weaning, offer your squirrels a variety of foods until you establish what they like to eat. Remember, just like any other animal, they need a varied and balanced diet if they are to stay healthy. All are different. I once had a grey squirrel that was passionate about digestive biscuits and fish fingers. She would actually climb down my arm and perch on my wrist just waiting for the fork to make contact with the plate. As soon as it did, she'd be down onto my hand like a flash and steal the morsel away to the safety of my shoulder for processing. More suitable squirrel foods are grains, nuts, berries, vegetables (especially cabbage and carrot), bread and fresh shoots. A good guide to how well your little squirrels are doing is weight. At the time their eyes open, red squirrels should weigh about 50g. (2oz.), and greys about 90g. (3oz.). By the time you are weaning them, reds should weigh about 150–170g. (5–6oz.) and greys about 200–220g. (7–8oz.).

A nest full of squirrels will become a house full of pests, so be warned. Squirrels tame well, and can give you hours of comical companionship, but they are very destructive (especially to picture rails and your best bit of Chippendale), noisy and can be unpredictable. Remember, they do bite, especially visitors whose scent is unfamiliar. After a few months they are big enough and so unreliable that it is unwise to keep them in the house. They are also heavy enough to dislodge ornaments and their claws can be quite dangerous. It is probably best to turn your orphans over to the local zoo or animal collection if you wish your house, children and friends to remain in one piece.

Older squirrels do not make very good patients, as they shock easily, and usually die before you can do anything to save them. Having said that, our local rector, a very keen naturalist, gave me a red squirrel that had been hit by a car recently. The squirrel had suffered a stroke, and was paralysed down one side. However, it just wouldn't give up. My vet gave it a multi-vitamin jab to help with the shock, and I bottle-fed it on glucose and water for three weeks until it was bouncing about again. It never regained the use of one front paw, but since I have seen grey squirrels manage admirably having lost a leg in a gamekeeper's trap, I have no reason to think that the squirrel didn't survive after we re-released it (well, to be honest, this squirrel made such a good recovery that it actually escaped from its convalescent enclosure).

Looking after sick and injured squirrels

Above all, think very carefully before taking injured squirrels into your care. Considering their cute and fluffy appearance, squirrels really are very tough cookies. After suffering the disappointment of ranks of little birds that failed to get well, despite my lavish attentions as a child, I was always of the opinion that trying to tend injured wild animals was really a very difficult task. Indeed one to be avoided if at all possible. However, squirrels present quite a different picture. Every injured character that I have tended has definitely displayed an unrivalled will to survive. As I write, I am in the process of caring for a 14-week-old female red squirrel, who has been completely disabled in a bump with a car, but who staunchly refuses to give up. Although her back legs do not work at all, she is remarkably mobile, dragging herself around with her front paws. She is alert, and will no doubt soon be a real menace in the house. But those appealing little eyes are irresistible as she guzzles her way through pipettefuls of invalid food, and dozens of almonds and walnuts every day.

You are most likely to find an injured squirrel that has picked an unsuccessful fight with a car. The first thing to say is handle your patient with extreme care. Prostrate it may be, badly wounded, or even unconscious . . . but, believe me, it can still bite. The best thing is to protect your hands with strong gloves, and avoid provoking the squirrel to take a chunk out of you. The things that they like least are to be squeezed around the ribs, to be held aloft with legs dangling (gives one the most dreadful sense of insecurity), or to be grabbed at with anything other than the gentleness that they deserve. Try encouraging the animal into a box or cloth bag, and then place it in a darkened room before examination. Squirrels behave much more calmly when sheltered from bright lights.

To start with, look for signs of shock. A shocked squirrel will sit on its haunches, or lie down, with its head tucked down against its tummy, and between its paws. It may well shake a good deal, close its eyes, and is oblivious to your prods and pokes. The best immediate medicine for shock is warmth. Don't boil the poor beast, but make sure that it is nice and warm. You might try getting the squirrel to take some glucose and water from a pipette before you move it too much. This will also help to counter shock.

It is usually best to pay a visit to your vet, particularly if he or she knows

you and your pets. Vets are generally sympathetic to cases of injury in wild animals, and the chap who thinks that you are wasting his time is very rare, so do go along and seek advice. Your vet will be able to identify any broken bones, and is really the best judge of whether it is worth trying to treat the squirrel, and look after it whilst its injuries heal. Your patient may need to have a leg set, or a wound stitched, or may simply require convalescence. In most cases, your vet will administer a jab for shock, a stock of vitamins to help the squirrel counter the trauma of its injuries, and probably some antibiotic if it has any open wounds. If you think that the patient is going to be difficult to feed at first, say if it is very weak, or very shy, it is probably best to ask for an injection of glucose and water under the skin, which will be slowly absorbed into the squirrel's blood stream over 24 hours. This will keep it going until you have tamed it sufficiently to allow pipette feeding.

Once you have embarked on the task of caring for your little furry friend whilst his wounds heal, the main things to remember are to keep the squirrel quiet, warm, and to feed small quantities regularly and often. You can keep your squirrel in a box or hamster cage, it won't really need space at this stage. A Pic-nic or freezer box is often very useful since it is insulated, keeping the heat in and has slippery sides that are difficult to climb. But do remember to have adequate ventilation. Good diets are standard invalid foods in liquid form that you can administer easly from a syringe minus its needle. Although often reluctant to feed from your hands, even adult squirrels will readily take to a pipette.

Squirrels get depressed very quickly if allowed to get dirty, so make sure that you keep the bedding meticulously clean, and, above all, dry. Each time you feed it, clean it thoroughly with cotton wool if it cannot clean itself. If your squirrel is only taking nourishment by pipette, it is bound to get a little runny behind, so don't worry. Try to offer solids in the form of hazel nuts, almonds (not sweetened or salted) or walnuts at every meal, and once your patient shows signs of taking solid food, try to build up the quantities daily until you can place a selection of nuts, berries and seeds in the cage or box ad-lib. I suggest that you continue pipette feeding until you are absolutely sure that the squirrel is fighting fit again. If in doubt, a return visit to your vet wouldn't go amiss. Don't forget to contact him and inform him of your progress anyway.

Once the injured squirrel begins to bounce, it can become a problem. No longer is it a quiet withdrawn little waif. Instead a lively, agile beast that can move with lightning speed and deliver a powerful bite to thank you for all your efforts. Squirrels hate to be unnecessarily confined, and there is no doubt that it is cruel to keep a wild adult squirrel yearning for its freedom. If you don't have an outdoor aviary in which your patient can complete a full convalescence, it's probably time to part company. In the case of a red squirrel, you should simply return it whence it came, and release it. For a grey the matter is a little more complex. Although you have done nothing wrong in caring for your squirrel, strictly speaking you would be breaking the law if you were to release it again into the wild because technically it is a pest species. It's probably best to contact your local Nature Conservancy Council office about what to do. Good luck!

Squirrel chow

The bits that they eat . . .

Squirrels are highly opportunistic creatures, and will make good use of any new food supply that becomes available, including the peanuts from your bird table, the bulbs from your spring border, and even the eggs from your chicken coop. However, their most important natural food is tree seed, including things like acorns and beech masts. This is where those lethal incisors come in. Trees would obviously prefer that their seeds were allowed to mature and get a chance to germinate, so they have developed an array of different mechanisms to protect them from becoming animal grub.

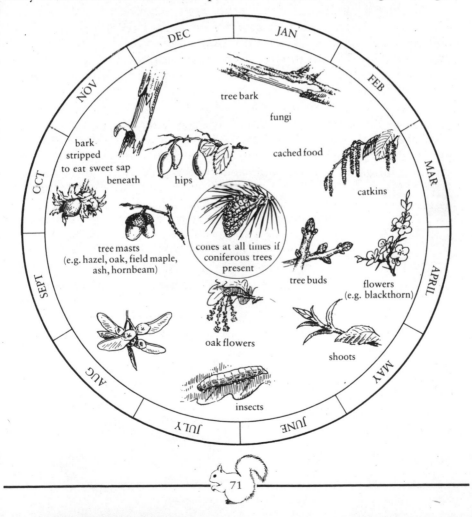

DEC — JAN — NOV — FEB — OCT — MAR — SEPT — APRIL — AUG — MAY — JULY — JUNE

tree bark

fungi

cached food

catkins

bark stripped to eat sweet sap beneath

hips

cones at all times if coniferous trees present

tree masts (e.g. hazel, oak, field maple, ash, hornbeam)

tree buds

flowers (e.g. blackthorn)

oak flowers

shoots

insects

The tiny seeds of coniferous trees are wrapped up in a tough cone, whilst deciduous trees like the hazel, beech and chestnut have thick coverings for their seeds which may provide protection against some beasts, but melt into insignificance in the face of a determined squirrel. Squirrels start to exercise their teeth on solid food before they are weaned. It does take a while to learn the finer points though, and the youngsters tend to travel about with Mum for the first week or so until they get the hang of things. Even then they can be pretty inexpert at handling food and in the event of a poor autumn seed crop, they may really suffer due to lack of experience.

Both red and grey squirrels spend most of their active time searching for, eating and storing food (see p.94). Indeed, nearly all of their travels are aimed at food gathering. Exactly what they eat depends largely upon where they live, and what is available. As you can imagine, the diet of a grey squirrel living beside the cafeteria in Regent's Park is likely to vary somewhat from that of a less cosmopolitan relation resident in the wilds of Wales. There is no major difference in the natural foods eaten by red and grey squirrels, although there may be some significant differences in their relative importance, and when they are eaten. For instance, in two oak woodlands under study on either side of the Solent in southern England, the response by grey squirrels to a poor acorn crop was to carry on looking for buried acorns, whilst red squirrels began feeding in the tree-tops on a fungus called *Vuilleminia* which grows under the bark of dead or dying oak branches: quite different ways of tackling the problem of food shortage.

Tree seeds come in a variety of shapes and sizes. Coniferous trees take a long time to develop the complex cones that envelop their seeds – in some cases, like the Monterey pine, over thirty years. This slow growth process means that developing, ripening and mature cones can be found amongst the canopy throughout most of the year. Where only one species of conifer is planted, squirrels may go hungry in the event of a complete cone crop failure, but in woods of mixed species, they can feed on cone seed nearly all the time.

Things are quite different in deciduous forests. Here tree seed production is highly seasonal, and the bulk of the crop ripens and falls in the autumn. So how do the squirrels cope? The same way you or I would if we were told that we could only go to Tesco once in the next twelve months . . . they fill the larder. Both red and grey squirrels store tree seed for future use by

(Right) *The red squirrel's agile body makes it well suited to clambering about among the fine tips of branches.*

burying it just below the surface of the soil and leaf litter in a cache. They tend to make a large number of caches, each comprising two or three articles, rather than storing all their food in one place, and this behaviour is called 'scatter hoarding'. Seeds are carried by mouth to a suitable burial ground, and are then pushed into a shallow hole excavated with the front paws. This hole is then covered up by a backwards scraping motion with the front paws, and finally the ground restored to its former glory by a firm push with the squirrel's nose.

Despite tree seed being just about the most important squirrel food, there are a whole host of other things that squirrels like to eat, most of which are seasonal. This means that instead of the squirrel's diet being a mix of different foods all the time, they tend to concentrate on each food in turn as it becomes available. This is particularly marked in deciduous woodland, where restriction of the seed season means that squirrels have to make better use of alternative foods. These include flowers, especially those of oak, buds, catkins, shoots, bark, sap, roots, ripening grains like wheat or barley (robbed from farmer Giles's fields next door to the wood) and fungus. It is also likely that squirrels pick up quite a number of insects whilst feeding amongst the canopy in summer, and they have been recorded eating carrion. Further dietary supplement may come from artificial foods, especially in the case of the city slickers. Squirrels have been recorded eating all sorts of unlikely things including plastic cable covering and all sorts of unmentionables . . . some more nutritious than others. Grey squirrels may become quite obese, much heavier than their country cousins. People also feed them deliberately, of course.

Do squirrels eat baby birds?

There is no doubt that there have been records of both red and grey squirrels taking nestling birds, and even taking them from nest boxes. However, it is unlikely that squirrels pose a serious threat to nesting birds. What is more likely is that they are simply taking advantage of the chance to vary their menu. During the spring and summer when most birds are raising their broods, squirrels may well be short of food. If one happens across a bowl full of inviting, if somewhat ghastly looking, steaks whilst foraging, it probably tucks in, but I have never seen any evidence that squirrels purposefully seek out bird's nests for a meal.

How do squirrels find their food?

Squirrels search for food using their eyes and their noses. In the case of tree seed, they search the canopy in a meticulous fashion, visiting the tips of all the branches and rummaging through the leaves for food. Red squirrels are superbly agile when it comes to feeding amongst fine twigs. They are light, and have proportionally longer legs than greys, making them well suited to delicate climbing. The animal usually clings to the twigs with the sharp

Squirrels often hang by their hind feet whilst they strip the bark from the underside of dead or dying oak branches in order to feed on fungi growing beneath.

claws on its hind feet, whilst reaching out for the tip of the branch with its front paws. This often involves dangling aloft, in a precarious position, being blown by the wind and rained upon ... the vertigo sufferer's nightmare. Once the food item has been detached from the tree, it is usually carried away to a safer place for eating. However, I have watched both red and grey squirrels with boundless confidence hanging upside down from tree branches by their hind feet whilst tucking into some tasty morsel or other.

Smell helps a squirrel find cached food buried under the leaf litter on the ground. Whilst searching, squirrels look like little Hoovers, hopping about with their faces pressed to the woodland floor. They can even do this through a thick layer of snow, as the tracks leading directly to holes and feeding remains will testify. It is highly unlikely, though, that squirrels can recognize caches that they themselves made the previous autumn. Many squirrels may cover the same piece of ground beneath the tree canopy, and bury their food there. Indeed, it is not uncommon to see several squirrels beavering away cacheing food within a few feet of one another. A squirrel returning weeks later will almost certainly dig up as many of his neighbour's hoards as he will his own. I have seen a female red squirrel feverishly

A cheeky youngster helping its mother to store food for the winter; (right) *a grey squirrel cacheing masts in the autumn.*

cacheing hazel nuts, making repeated journeys to and from the canopy to collect them. She was followed at a discreet distance by one of her offspring, who promptly dug them all up again and wolfed the lot.

How to tell a good nut from a bad one

If you examine the ground beneath a hazel tree where a squirrel has been feeding, amongst the discarded shells, you will undoubtedly find some whole nuts that have been thrown away intact. Open the nuts, and, nine times out of ten, the kernel is withered or absent altogether. So how did the squirrel know not to bother opening that particular nut if it has clearly not even gnawed a small hole in the shell to look inside?

If you watch squirrels handling nuts, they clasp them between the palms of their front paws, and rotate them several times with the toes and claws before starting to feed. Experiments with shells, some empty and others full of lead shot, would seem to indicate that the squirrel is testing the weight of the nut, and will only try to open it if it is heavy. A nut with a withered kernel will be considerably lighter than one with a good seed, and squirrels are obviously quite good at sorting out the duds. The ability to test weight in this fashion must save a lot of time and be a useful way of saving energy for the foraging squirrel.

The bits that they leave

Once a squirrel has found its food, it then has to remove all the extraneous bits in order to get a meal. These extra bits are discarded and can be used to help indicate both what squirrels have been eating and where. Seeds in cones are tiny, and come in an extravagant package that requires quite considerable determination and skill to unlock. Squirrels hold cones between their front paws, with the tip of the cone in one paw, and the butt end in the other. In this respect, they may be either left- or right-handed, each animal seemingly always holding the cone tip in the same paw. The cone is then rotated as the squirrel bites off the bracts and cone scales until it finds a seed. When it does, it lets go of the cone with one paw, and puts the seed into its mouth before continuing onto the next seed. Once all the scales have been removed, and the seeds eaten, the cone core is discarded. Stripped cone cores can be found all over the floor of a coniferous forest, with the scales strewn about them. They have not always been stripped by squirrels though, and care must be taken not to confuse the cleanly stripped 'squirrelled' cone with the frayed and chewed 'birded' cone, shredded by crossbills, for example. Squirrels aren't dumb either; they will reject any cones that do not provide sufficient return for their efforts, for example those with very small seeds, or without any at all, so don't be surprised if not every cone has all the scales removed.

Acorns have a tough covering that can be peeled off using the incisor

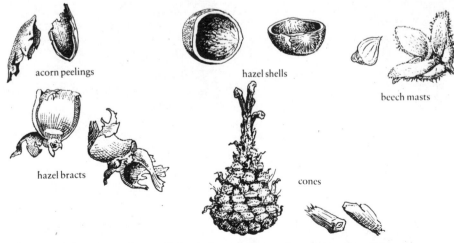

acorn peelings

hazel shells

beech masts

hazel bracts

cones

An assortment of the leftovers from the squirrel's table.

teeth, but hazel nuts require a bit more skill. The nut is held between the palms, and is rotated using the long toes and claws until the point is upwards. The squirrel than bites a neat hole into the top of the nut, and inserts the incisor teeth before prising the two halves of the shell apart (see p.36). You can often pick up the shells of hazel nuts opened by squirrels and fit the two halves of one nut together perfectly. Walnuts and almonds are tackled in a similar fashion, although the softer sweet chestnut is peeled rather like an acorn, and the shredded bits of brown skin scattered around beneath where the squirrel was feeding. Despite being large and appetizing-looking seeds, conkers don't seem to be eaten; they taste horribly bitter to me, so perhaps that's what puts the squirrels off too.

Not all squirrel foods come in hard casings. A walk through a forest in the spring when the young shoots are sprouting may reveal the tattered remains of fresh foliage on the ground. The squirrel has been eating the growing tips of the shoots before they harden, and discarding the majority of the new leaves. Under oak trees, bunches of young leaves, sometimes with a piece of the twig still attached indicate that a squirrel has been feeding on shoot tips and flowers. The squirrel bites off the new leaf sprig and removes only the central growing point, young stems and flowers before chucking the rest . . . it looks terribly wasteful, but doesn't seem to damage the trees. The same treatment is given to the catkins of hazel and birch, and the flowers of a number of species, including blackthorn, ash and even horse chestnut.

Fungi are often carried off to be eaten or stored in the canopy, but occasionally a sharp eyed observer can find larger fungi bearing squirrel teeth marks. I have found such marks on a whole variety of fungi including some that are very good to eat like wood blewits and parasol mushrooms (the squirrels must have stood on tip toe), but also on some pretty ghastly examples like panther caps and death caps. It would be interesting to know whether they survived to sample another meal.

Bark stripping for food is common among squirrels. Both reds and greys strip the bark of dead oak branches to scrape off fungi growing underneath. This behaviour leaves piles of small pieces of bark on the ground, and a clean, bright stripped patch on the bough. They may also eat the bark itself, which turns up as a component of the diet almost all the year round . . . no roughage problems here. Both species also strip the bark of living trees and scrape off the soft juicy sappy tissue below, leaving characteristic teeth marks all over the wood.

Why do squirrels strip bark?

The anti-social habit of bark stripping by squirrels is the bane of every forester's life. It gets the squirrels into deep trouble, and millions of pounds have been spent on squirrel eradication programmes in an effort to save plantations from damage. Indeed, the wry conclusion of one recent piece of

Squirrels strip the bark of some trees in order to eat the sweet sap below.

research into the problem was that future efforts should be directed towards perfecting recipes for squirrel pie.

Squirrels strip tree bark with their incisor teeth. The damage is done by them peeling off tree bark in order to eat the juicy sap layer below. Trouble usually starts with a number of small trial strips being removed, but, if conditions are right, huge areas of bark may be peeled off. If the stripped area joins up around the trunk, this is called 'ring barking'. By removing all the sap layer in a complete ring around the tree, the squirrel has effectively made a break in the tree's plumbing, and sap can no longer pass up and down the trunk. Thus, everything above the chewed ring in the bark will be deprived of water and nutrients from the soil, and will consequently die. A tree ring barked near the ground will succumb to autumn storms and fall over, whilst one damaged near the top will lose its crown, and be stunted. Even if the squirrels don't ring bark a tree, stripped patches are vulnerable to insect and fungal attack, and may form calluses that spoil the tree's timber value.

There have been many theories as to why squirrels strip tree bark. Could it be compulsive gnawing? Maybe it's to keep their incisors worn down since there is little other hard food about in the summer? Perhaps they are just short of food. These theories do not explain why stripping may occur when squirrel numbers are low, when there is supplementary food provided, or why the problem may be localized, and bad in one year, but not the next. Recent research has shown that the most likely reason for squirrel bark stripping is that the creatures simply like to eat the sweet sap below. This is borne out by the fact that trees prone to stripping tend to be young (with relatively soft bark) vulnerable species like sycamore, beech and pine, which have sweet sap. Favoured trees also have the thickest sap layer, which the squirrel tests with its trial strips, and trees without thick sap layers are rarely damaged. Hence damage may be localized (restricted to sappy trees only), and may also be worse in one year (particularly if growing conditions are ideal and the sap is rising fast) than in the next. This theory that squirrel damage is linked to tree quality also supports the forester's lament that the wretched squirrels always damage the best trees. These are the ones that will be growing most vigorously because they have a lovely thick layer of sweet sap. Sadly, both species of squirrel are equally guilty.

Unfortunately, once a squirrel has acquired the habit of bark stripping, it is unlikely to forget the resultant tasty meal. Some young squirrels probably learn from Mum whilst following her about. In other cases, stripping may be triggered by an aggressive encounter. Summer, when most damage occurs, is the time when spring-born young are first out and about, causing a sharp rise in squirrel density. If things get a bit overcrowded, squirrels will chew bark in a 'huff'. The pleasant surprise of a sweet sappy meal could then encourage further investigation and hence more serious damage. Indeed, there is evidence that good squirrel breeding in the spring, combined with favourable tree-growing weather, is likely to herald disastrous bark stripping. Perhaps in the event of such conditions, the forester's nerves would benefit from a summer holiday.

Do squirrels drink?

Squirrels get most of the water that they require from their diet. They eat a lot of moist vegetable matter of one form or another, and frequently forage in dew-soaked surroundings where they cannot avoid water. However, they do also drink, although this behaviour is seldom seen in the wild.

Wild squirrels drink from water-filled hollows in tree-trunks, and from small puddles trapped in leaves. If the edge of a pond or stream is close to woodland it may also be visited, particularly in warm weather. Grey squirrels are well known for their bold, outgoing behaviour, and they frequently visit garden pools and bird baths for a drink. Indeed, I have seen them drink from fountain pools in a public park, whilst being viewed by hordes of tourists.

Squirrels in the garden

If you live in the countryside, and your garden is close to woodland, you will almost certainly be visited by inquisitive squirrels. In some parts of the country, you may be lucky enough to see red squirrels, but in most places you will find greys. Although most people would be delighted to have a regular red squirrel visitor, greys seem to elicit a wide range of responses; everything from hampers full of peanuts to shotguns.

In many European cities, red squirrels are a common sight in urban gardens, but not so in all parts of this country. It was not always this way. Even as recently as forty years ago, red squirrels were frequent visitors to our parks and town gardens. In some places this still occurs, however, as their numbers have gradually dwindled, we see fewer and fewer of them outside large undisturbed forests. Grey squirrels, on the other hand, are the bold American temperament personified. They occupy many town parks, and few gardens escape their attention, especially if they sport a well stocked bird table.

There is no doubt that squirrels, be they red or grey, bring an enormous amount of pleasure to most garden watchers. However, they can be a bit of

a menace at times, and I have had desperate telephone calls from folk trying to evict them. One problem is that squirrels will insist on stripping the bark from your favourite ornamental tree, just as it was turning out to be a good'un. As we have seen, there are complex reasons behind bark stripping by squirrels in the wild, but in your garden, the most likely cause is straightforward aggression. Providing food for your neighbourhood squirrels tends to concentrate them around your garden, and the resulting bad tempers at such close proximity may be vented upon the nearest chewable object. If you watch carefully, an aggressive encounter between two squirrels is nearly always followed up by some sort of 'huffy' behaviour, say avid grooming, or, frequently, bark chewing.

Another squirrel misdemeanour is to dig little holes all over your bowling green lawn. The prudent squirrel responds to your deluge of bird table grub by rushing around and burying as much as it can. They will usually secrete their caches somewhere a bit more private, like the herbaceous border, but the boldest of your visitors will cheerfully use the centre of the lawn in full view of the world.

Bulb digging is another irritating squirrel pastime. The devastation of your spring border may be an indirect result of food cacheing activities, although that is of no comfort to our budding Percy Thrower. Squirrels do eat bulbs, and the oversized cultivars that we place in the ground (specifically for their delight, you understand) can prove irresistible to a hungry visitor.

How to attract squirrels to your garden

Squirrels may come to your gardens for a number of reasons. An over-zealously mown lawn will provide a very good source of moss for nest lining. Your garden pond may be the most easily attainable drink on a hot summer's day. And, of course, with a bit of modification, the nest box that you intended for a bird will make a good squirrel home. However, the biggest attraction to any garden visitor is *food*.

Squirrels will quite happily pillage the nuts and seeds from your bird table, but this can cause problems. For one thing, most birds will be frightened off by a squirrel on the rampage, and, for another, the wretched table will need stocking three or four times a day. Not only this, but squirrels are so ingenious that it is no good trying to hide food in hanging baskets or nets specially for the birds. You will find that your squirrels very soon cotton on to this ploy and can remove food from even the most precariously balanced hopper. They will even dangle upside down by their toes in order to steal bird food from hanging nets, or may simply pull up the string from which the basket is suspended until the goal is achieved. I know one lady who puts out nets of peanuts for the birds in her garden, only to watch them being massacred by red squirrels which chew holes in the nets within minutes. If you want to watch both squirrels and birds, it is probably advisable to feed them at separate tables. You can make a squirrel-proof bird table quite easily, because squirrels can't fly, and therefore have to either jump onto or climb up your construction in order to reach the goal. A slippery pole with a squirrel proof collar (see diagram) stops them from climbing up onto the table, and placing it out in the open deprives the squirrel of a perch from which to jump. On the other hand, your special

squirrel table should be placed near a hedge, bushes or a tree, and can usefully be attached to the latter. I even know of one keen red squirrel watcher who observed his red visitors having trouble getting onto his bird table, so he built them a special one at ground level. The danger here is that your intended visitor may fall prey to next door's marauding Tom.

Squirrels will eat a whole variety of foods, but it is a good idea to keep your offerings as natural as possible. Some research suggests that certain of the more common garden baits can be bad for squirrels. For instance,

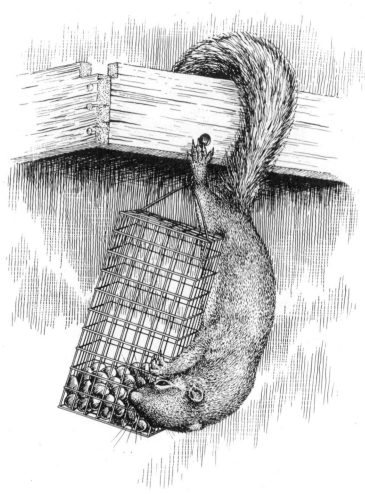

Squirrels soon learn to take advantage of extra food offerings.

A squirrel-proof bird table.

peanuts contain high levels of phosphorus, which can inhibit the absorption of calcium in the squirrel's gut. If youngsters learn to visit your table, and rely upon a source of peanuts only, they may develop rickets because their growing bones are not getting enough calcium. Equally, sweet foods like sultanas and raisins can have the same effect if eaten to excess.

It is best to feed a whole variety of different foods, similar to those that the squirrel might encounter in the wild, with added extras in small amounts. Grains like wheat or whole maize will be taken by grey squirrels and make cheap squirrel table foods. Hazel nuts are superb if you can afford them, so too are beech nuts and sweet chestnuts. Only feed small quantities of oily seeds like those of sunflowers and peanuts, and I would avoid preserved fruits altogether. At the back of the book, I have provided an address from which you can obtain the squirrel bait that I have been using for the past few years, with no ill effects. It honestly looks good enough to eat for your own breakfast.

Feeding squirrels

Now this is a difficult one. You must think of the animals, rather than just your own pleasure in seeing them. My own observations indicate that squirrels can be drawn some considerable distance by a food table; some will travel more than a kilometre for a daily meal. However, they do not generally give up natural foraging and rely entirely upon supplementary food. Some weakling youngsters can become quickly dependent upon your bird table, and they are particularly vulnerable to events like summer holidays, and the subsequent lack of grub.

Most people think that the winter is the hardest time for squirrels, all that frost and snow. However, they actually reach their peak weight of the year in January. In fact, if the tree seed and mast crop has been good, squirrels are unlikely to be hungry over the winter months at all, because they can utilize all the grub that they buried in the autumn. However, if there were very few seeds and nuts for them in the autumn, your squirrel table could be vital during the subsequent winter. Only squirrels that are well fed over the winter will breed in the spring, and in the event of a natural seed crop failure (say there were few acorns, hazel or pine cones), there may be no spring litters at all. Thus it is best to gauge your winter feeding according to the natural food availability. If it seems like a fruitful autumn, feed lightly over the winter. On the contrary, if finding hazel nuts in the autumn is like the veritable needle in a hay stack, indulge your garden visitors a bit.

Summer is more frequently a hard time for squirrels. If you think about it, there isn't a lot about for them to eat. Once they have polished off the young buds, shoots and flowers, they are left with searching for leftover caches, and any fresh young greenery available. In my red squirrel studies, it was during the summer that most deaths occurred as animals succumbed to starvation. On top of the food shortage problem, this is also the time of year when female squirrels have young, and those that have been weaned must learn to fend for themselves. Feeding squirrels at your table in the height of summer might seem illogical, but you will probably be doing them more of a service than providing winter supplements. Be careful, though. You don't want to encourage those babies to spend all their time on your table, and none at all learning to fend for themselves. It is best to feed small amounts every three or four days. This way, you may provide enough help to keep the squirrels alive until the more bountiful autumn, but you will not encourage them into bad habits, like lurking in the bush under the table and never straying more than a few metres from your garden.

The three-dimensional world of squirrels

Squirrels make full use of the three-dimensional environment provided by woodland. They are at home in the tree tops, lower down amongst bushes and shrubs, or on the woodland floor itself. Indeed, the high concentrations of light-sensitive cells in a squirrel's eye give it acute vision specialized for judging distances in a vertical (up and down) world. Squirrels are also superb climbers, and can travel from the canopy to the ground (or vice versa) in a fast and seemingly effortless glide, clinging to tree bark like a speeding, furry limpet. Squirrels certainly seem more at home in the tree tops. They move about with great agility, and can perform daring leaps, hang by their toes whilst chomping nuts, and have a good wash and brush-up whilst balanced in some precarious seat up in the heavens. On the ground, they are generally more cautious, especially red squirrels. Their gait is a strange stilted hop with tail outstretched. It is quite slow, and interrupted by frequent stops to stand bolt upright and sniff the air for danger. The slightest movement, or whiff of trouble and they're off, bounding across the ground to the nearest tree. It is most likely this slow and rather ungainly movement on the ground that allows so many squirrels to fall prey to domestic dogs and cats.

Squirrels are very good at jumping, and use their large tails as rudders whilst leaping.

A comparison of red (left) *and grey* (right) *squirrel arboreality.*

Making use of the vertical component of their surroundings means that when we measure the space used by squirrels, in terms of an area on a map, we are not really taking into account the true space that the animal occupies. That space is not flat, but more like the inside of a big box: it has depth as well as length and breadth. How they use that volume of space provides one of the most interesting comparisons between red and grey squirrels.

Woodland is a bountiful place. There is squirrel food to be had in the canopy, in the form of shoots, buds, flowers, insects and developing seeds. On the way down to the ground, there is a meal of bark, fungi, honeysuckle flowers or perhaps some greenery or nuts from woodland shrubs. When you reach the ground, there's more fungi, fallen goodies from above, buried caches, bulbs and, in town, the well intentioned squirrel feeder. There's a lot to choose from. It would appear from recent behavioural studies, that red and grey squirrels go about making a meal of that lot in quite different ways. Grey squirrels spend a great deal of their time on the ground, and will quite boldly search for food right out in the open, unprotected by cover, and often well away from the nearest tree. Red squirrels, on the other hand, spend most of their time feeding up in the tree canopy. This difference is very marked, and clearly the two species can't be feeding on the same things at the same times, although the lists of food they eat are identical.

To a certain extent, we could have predicted these behavioural differences when looking at the body structure of the two species. Re squirrels are significantly lighter than greys, but with a frame very similar in size. Light weight in proportion to body size is one characteristic of tree-dwelling mammals. Another adaptation is long powerful limbs specialized for climbing and leaping. In comparison with grey squirrels, reds have much longer limbs in proportion to their weight. Overall, these differences in body structure amount to something like a comparison between a steeplechaser and a draught horse. Strip them both of skin and muscle, and they look much the same. But in the flesh, you would never expect the draught horse to leap high fences, or the steeplechaser to deliver your beer. The red squirrel's slender build probably makes it significantly more agile in tree tops, whilst the heavier grey is undoubtedly better able to dig into frozen soil and recover a food supply buried months previously.

What conclusions can we draw from these physical and behavioural differences between reds and greys? It is clear that they are different, and not just in shape and size. The more information that is collected from detailed study of their behaviour, the more apparent the differences become. What would seem to be emerging is the fact that red and grey squirrels use different strategies to exploit the resources available in their environment, particularly food. The subtle differences in their body shape have evolved over millions of years as adaptations to a particular way of life; a specific way of doing things. The most important question is, do those differences mean that one is better off than the other? Were one strategy more efficient than the other, then one species could possibly be in trouble when co-existing with the other. This could well be part of the answer to the red/grey story, where one *is* successful and the other seems to be in dire trouble.

Gadding about

Why do squirrels go out?
Behavioural studies have shown that the main reason why any squirrel stirs its stumps is food. They do sundry other activities whilst out and about, including sex, grooming and falling asleep, but few things apart from food occupy much of the squirrel's time. So squirrels are active whilst they are hungry, and, unless there is something pressing, like a mate, to keep them out of bed, they probably just return there as soon as they are full.

A most common glimpse of a wild red squirrel.

When are squirrels active?
As a rule, squirrels are active every day. Yes, *every day*, even in the winter, for tree squirrels do not hibernate. Just look for the tracks in the snow to prove it. Unlike the ground squirrels (see p.13) and animals like dormice, tree squirrels do not have the ability to store huge amounts of fat in order to stay alive through long periods of winter sleep. They do put on weight for the winter, but they just get tubby, not obese. This means that a couple of days without food, and the reserve tanks are running low, with starvation looming around the corner. So squirrels have to be active on most days. Severe cold, heavy rain, high winds, or a strong heatwave may keep them at home for a day, or at most two, but this means living dangerously because they can't survive long without food.

Having said that, winter activity is minimal. Grey squirrels are only active for between one and three hours on winter mornings (they usually rise at dawn), although research indicates that red squirrels may be active for much longer. In summer the days are long, and food may be scarce. The result is that squirrels tend to be out searching for food all day. However, a squirrel's stomach isn't very big, and the food available at that time of the year is often quite bulky and of low nutritional value, such as shoots, buds and bark. The result is a pattern of activity which starts at dawn, and is broken by one or more siestas as the squirrel digests a stomachful before resuming the search. I have often recorded red squirrels up before dawn, and foraging on until the last vestiges of light when you can hardly see a hand in front of your face.

How far do squirrels travel?
Just try following one. To the casual observer it may seem that there is a squirrel in every tree, and another bouncing across every grassy glade. But if you actually try and follow a squirrel, all you will witness is a series of miraculous disappearing acts. It would be extremely difficult to make a study of squirrel movements without some help. This is where radio-tracking comes in.

Being one of the more recent generation of field biologists, I can only imagine that life without radio-tracking must have been sheer hell. It is still

A radio-tagged red squirrel alert whilst foraging on the ground.

an expensive pastime. A basic set-up, with ten squirrel tags (special collars on which are mounted miniature radio transmitters which continually broadcast the animal's position for up to six months), a special receiver capable of tuning into the high frequency band allocated to wildlife research by the Home Office, and a directional antenna (to indicate where the signal is coming from) will cost you about £1,200. These prices may well rule out the use of radio-tracking in many student projects. So it's quite likely that the cost of equipment is a serious limiting factor on the progress of good research. Some inventive souls may cut the price by making their own tags, but this is often fraught with problems, and takes a great deal of practice.

Despite these setbacks, most of the recent research on squirrels in Britain has been carried out with the help of radio-tracking. Each study animal is fitted with a miniature transmitter powered by a lithium battery that will last for about nine months. After that, the transmitter is fitted with a new battery and is ready to go again. This package is carried on a light brass collar worn around the squirrel's neck. Fitted properly, these collars have no detectable effect upon the animal's behaviour. After all, there would be no point in studying a beast that was not behaving normally because it was carrying a ball and chain. In fact, the collars weigh less than 5 per cent of the squirrel's body; lighter in proportion to their weight than many women's handbags (well, big handbags).

With a good receiver and directional antenna, the squirrel tags that I use can be picked up well over a kilometre (half a mile) away from the animal. This can be useful. Firstly, you know where the squirrel is long before it can see or hear you, so you can creep up quietly and find it without causing a disturbance. Secondly, squirrels can make quite spectacular movements, and a transmitter with a long range then becomes essential. For instance, when I was working as a research assistant studying grey squirrels, some young animals that we tagged left their birth place and travelled in excess of ten miles in only a few days. We actually had to take the receiver up in an aircraft to find them. I have never recorded such movements in radio-tagged red squirrels, although on the Continent they are known to migrate many tens of kilometres in the event of severe food shortage, and daily movements of just under one kilometre are not uncommon.

On the whole, male squirrels tend to travel more than females, particularly during the breeding season. They pick up the smell of a female on heat, and will make long journeys to join in a mating chase. In contrast, a female squirrel with young in her drey will often travel no more than a few tens of metres from them during the first weeks of their lives.

If you study a squirrel's movements over a number of days, or preferably weeks, you will soon build up a picture of the general area that it normally occupies. Biologists like to call this the animal's 'home-range', although it is a pretty dubious term since there are no hard and fast rules about how to define it. What we mean is the place occupied by a squirrel , which is roughly the same year after year, although the boundaries of their general range vary considerably. We must also be clear not to confuse 'range' and 'territory'. A territory is a piece of space that an animal actively defends by chasing away all intruders, and displaying aggressively. British squirrels do not do this (except perhaps a female directly after her litter has been born, who will chase away intruders from the drey tree) and should not be considered territorial beasts. Young squirrels have tiny ranges to start with, centred upon their litter drey. However, as they grow, they start to move about a bit, and if they eventually move away from their parents' wood, may make some enormous journeys. Squirrel ranges overlap, particularly at times of food abundance when they all cram into the best trees to feed. But they do seem to have a distinct pecking order, and woe betide any upstart who seeks to defy it. Red squirrels tend to have bigger ranges than greys probably because they live at a lower density, and animals don't waste space or resources. You would expect an average grey squirrel to occupy about 7 ha, whilst a red of similar age and status would use about 8 ha during an average year. But it is very difficult to generalize about these things.

The boundary of a squirrel's range varies considerably with the season. Their movements tend to be decisive. Rather than dawdling, they will travel to a good feeding place, feed, and then travel on to the next, or back to the drey. Travelling bouts are frequently broken by grooming sessions and the odd stop for a sniff, but all conducted at high speed. In deciduous woodland ranges tend to contract during the summer when grub is in short supply. It would seem that it is better to conserve energy by moving about as little as possible, and search every last twig, rather than to dash about and find nothing. Indeed, they will often spend most of a hot summer's day searching one tree crown for flowers or young seeds, moving no more than a few metres in total. At this time of year it is not unusual for a squirrel to move only a few hundred metres (yards) in a day. In the autumn when seeds are ripening, ranges may expand dramatically. The feeding pattern at this time of the year is frenzied, with frantic searching of twigs, whilst moving rapidly through the canopy. Only when the squirrel finds a well ripened tree will it stop and feed in between repeated trips to the ground in order to cache seeds. The whole scene looks a bit like a speeded up Keystone Cops chase and, in contrast to the summer feeding pattern, squirrels may travel in excess of several kilometres in a single day. During the winter, male ranges may expand as they begin to search for mates. Frequently one male's range will overlap those of several females at this time.

Can squirrels swim?

Yes, they can. Squirrels frequently visit open water to drink during hot weather, and, in the course of their travels, will undoubtedly come across water on many occasions. It is doubtful that they intentionally go for a swim — after all, what would be the reason? However, I have twice seen hapless squirrels which have fallen into water, having to swim to safety. They swim with the body submerged, and only the head (with very disturbed expression) above water. When once more upon terra firma, they don't look like natural water-lovers, more like dejected drowned rats with rather odd tails.

Squirrel social life

Are squirrels sociable? Well, British squirrels certainly are not territorial, and the space that they normally occupy will invariably overlap with that of several other squirrels. But do they 'get along' with one another? They certainly seem to have quite distinct 'pecking orders' whereby more dominant animals chase subordinates, who just run away rather than standing up for themselves.

As infants, squirrels only have contact with their mothers. Their fathers are present at conception, but that's about it. Squirrels never form stable pairs, although one female may mate with the same male for a number of years, purely by virtue of the fact that their ranges overlap. The female will nurse her young, clean them up, give them her fleas and generally fuss about them until they are about ten weeks old, when they begin to venture out and about. For a short while, the female and her young form a sort of small family, all sticking quite close together. Like most young animals, baby squirrels are very playful, and will occupy themselves for hours in rough and tumble games. But their contact with Mum and brothers and sisters gradually reduces during the first few weeks of independence, and, after that, they are on their own.

A squirrel marking its regular routeway by face wiping.

Grey squirrel chattering.

Squirrels announce themselves by scent marking. They urinate on small pieces of stripped bark and on regularly used routeways. They also wipe their faces on tree branches. This is in order to deposit a smelly secretion from a glandular lip plate as a sort of calling card. This behaviour suggests that probably the chief way that squirrels recognize one another is by smell. And leaving your own personal smell about the place is a way of marking out your space, even though this space is not defended. Each squirrel simply reminds others of its presence by scent marking. There is also some evidence that individuals might avoid one another by visiting good food patches in their overlapping ranges at different times, usually scent marking somewhere as they leave.

The older and more senior squirrels in a wood have usually been living in one patch for a number of years. They get to know the smell of near neighbours, and will tolerate them without too much chasing about. Any new youngster must be faced with a barrage of strange smells as it moves away from Mum's area, and, should it meet any of the smell's owners, it will probably be chased away as an unrecognized stranger. This is why youngsters are often found relegated to the worse bits of the wood, where nobody else wants to live. They're the only places where they don't get chased. As the older squirrels die off, the younger members of the population (if they have survived their banishment) manage to slip into better habitat and establish a more permanent space.

Occasionally tension can lead to fights. Situations like a cheeky youngster persisting in making a nuisance of itself, two dominant animals meeting on 'home-ground', possibly when a wandering adult strays into a local dominant's patch, or when males vie for a female's attentions may provoke a fight. This is a nasty business, accompanied by much chattering and screaming, and frequently involving the loss of toes, ears and chunks of body. This is obviously undesirable, and squirrels usually defuse aggression and avoid fights by posturing furiously at one another in an attempt to establish supremacy. After all, there's no point in getting bitten if you don't have to.

We don't know very much about squirrel social structure. What we do know is that dominant animals usually are the older and heavier ones, and youngsters are at the bottom of the pile. However, in my study of red squirrels on the Isle of Wight it was the females that were usually most dominant, whilst in a Belgian study of the same species, it was the males. Possibly a bit of the old Britannia coming out here.

Do reds and greys mix?

Conventional wisdom says that the replacement of reds by grey squirrels is the result of the hideous, violent grey gobbling up all the reds. Sorry, folks, this just isn't true. Both squirrels scent mark, and their loose social structures are much the same. In studies of interactions between the two species, it would appear that there are no more fights between reds and greys than there are between reds alone or greys alone. So if you are a poor, persecuted red squirrel, you are just as likely to lose a toe at the tooth of another red as you are to have it bitten off by a filthy rotten foreigner. At Regent's Park, where they recently released red squirrels into the zoo grounds, greys were a wee bit more likely to win a fight with a red, except in the close proximity of the weight selective feed hoppers (see p.114) specifically designed for the reds. Here, a red squirrel was more likely to knock hell out of a marauding grey . . . so there!

Furthermore, red and grey squirrels living in the same wood will occupy one another's dreys. They have never been recorded sleeping in the same drey at the same time, but at different times. This is most probably how red squirrels pick up grey squirrel fleas and vice versa.

Squirrel talk

Squirrels are expressive little beasts. It's part of what makes them so appealing. To start with, they have a comprehensive collection of squeaks, chirrs, grunts and squeals with which to liven up the woods. Youngsters are often the most vocal, letting out squeals when they get into a fix, and constantly chittering at one another during play. Adults are more selective, and their calls are mostly associated with meeting other squirrels, or being disturbed, particularly by us.

Red and grey squirrels sound quite different. The grey squirrel utters a slightly metallic *chirr* when disturbed, much more uniform than the explosion of *chik-chik-chik-chirrrrrr*, a very staccato call from a disgruntled red squirrel. These alarm calls are often accompanied by a sort of teeth chattering that will invariably continue until either you go away or the squirrel goes off in a huff. There is also a call, first noted by Monica Shorten in her book about squirrels, associated with mating. I have heard a female red squirrel give this cry – *chik-chik-chik-chik-ooooeeeeee*, a most mournful wail – whilst chasing males were in the vicinity. Since these courtship affairs can often be long drawn out (see p.59), the call may serve to spur the males on.

Squirrels don't just talk with their voices. Indeed, their body language is often far more expressive. Just about the most important squirrel signal post is its tail. When subdued or snoozing, its huge bushy tail is generally held over its back and head umbrella style. On the move, it is either held out behind the animal, or used as a rudder when jumping. But as a communication flag, it leaps into much more vigorous action. Tail flagging, or flicking, can mean a number of things. When a squirrel is disturbed or defensive, it will repeatedly flick its tail up and down whilst uttering a slow *chuk-chuk-chuk*. This is often accompanied by 'tree-slapping', when the animal slaps the tree bark with its feet in jerky movements. The whole picture is of a very aggravated squirrel. Tail flagging is also used as a sort of greeting, or warning to other squirrels, the pace of flicking increasing as the animal gets more and more cross.

Tail swishing – a sweeping side-to-side movement – generally means that the squirrel is not quite sure of the situation. Vigorous swishing often occurs just before the squirrel makes a difficult leap, or when it is not certain whether it saw you down there or not.

For anyone who has to catch squirrels in order to mark, weigh or tag them, youngsters are a real nuisance. As soon as you touch them, they

squeal for Mum and make a terrible fuss, a bit like that irritating little cry-baby in your class at school. On one occasion when I was handling a young grey squirrel, Mum actually appeared on the scene in answer to its cries. I can only say that the ensuing performance was a bit of everything I have just talked about all rolled into one. What's more, the female got so cross that she began to chew bark in between cursing and swearing at me. The falling pieces gave one the distinct impression that as well as doling out expletives, she was also trying to hurl things at me.

How many squirrels are there?

The size and density of populations of shy and elusive creatures are very difficult to assess. You certainly wouldn't get far by just counting squirrels seen. Firstly, they are so difficult to see, and then you have the problem of telling one from another so you don't count anyone twice. There are all sorts of problems with trying to relate the number of squirrels to the number of dreys, and squirrels don't leave convenient markers like paths or latrines. Basically, if you want to count them, you need to catch and mark them.

Biologists have devised ways of counting difficult animals using methods of capture, mark and re-capture. By marking all the individuals in a trapped sample, releasing them, and then re-capturing a second sample, and comparing the numbers of marked individuals with the first, you can estimate the population size . . . honest, guv. This method works quite well for things like periwinkles where you can easily catch a lot of animals in one sample, but for squirrels? Well, they like live traps, and are easily caught time and time again. Some of them actually get 'trap-happy', and you more or less have to prise them out of your traps with a crowbar. But you have to put out an awful lot of traps, and walk a very long way in order to get a big enough sample number to estimate population size. It can be done, it just involves hours of time, miles of walking and huge sackfuls of bait.

Despite the fact that red and grey squirrels have the potential to produce equal numbers of young every year, live as long as one another, and usually die of the same things, their population densities are radically different. Somewhere something goes wrong. You will frequently find grey squirrels living at three or four times the density of reds in exactly the same type of habitat. This would seem to indicate that somehow grey squirrels are better at fulfilling their potential, at breeding successfully and at surviving, than our native red squirrel. It also helps to explain how greys replace reds. With a low breeding success, and low survival rates, red squirrels are very vulnerable to invasion by a species that can breed faster, and whose young survive better, particularly in the event of some sort of environmental hardship. However, we should be cautious in naming poor breeding and survival as a *cause* of replacement. Poor breeding in itself is an effect of the squirrels being hungry, overcrowded, or diseased; it is in this direction that we need to look for causes of the red squirrel's demise.

Squirrel population levels fluctuate seasonally. Each time a new crop of youngsters, which biologists call a 'cohort' (like a year set at school), comes along, the population swells. Eventually that increase will be levelled by deaths, both of young and old squirrels, and in between times we have other individuals coming and going, and possibly staying. This means that both seasonal and yearly fluctuations are marked. In a good year with plenty of food about and nice weather, red squirrels may reach a density of just over 1 per hectare, or 1 every two and a half acres of woodland. Greys in the same type of habitat could be living at a density of 4 per hectare. In a bad year, red squirrel population density could sink as low as 0.5 per hectare or 1 every 5 acres, and greys maybe to about 2 per hectare.

One question that I am always asked is, 'How many red squirrels are there on the Isle of Wight?' Well, there are 4,100 hectares of woodland on the island, so in a good year, there could be 4,100 red squirrels, and in a bad year, only 2,050. Such an estimate of numbers is pretty meaningless, though. What difference would it make if there were 4,101 instead of 4,100? And this also assumes that squirrel density is the same in all woods regardless of type. Clearly a localized estimate of population density tells you much more about the squirrels, since you take into account the surroundings and other factors which might have an effect. A calculation of the population size – say, in Britain – with all its inherent assumptions, is really no use at all.

Handling squirrels

I am sure that every child who has read Beatrix Potter would love to cuddle Squirrel Nutkin. However, squirrels are not at all easy to handle, especially when cross or injured.

People who regularly feed and handle squirrels in local parks will probably be horrified that I should suggest that their beloved friends could be the perpetrators of such wicked damage to humankind. But the fact remains that the average squirrel will not appreciate being picked up, let alone cuddled, so for the most part I should approach them with a healthy respect.

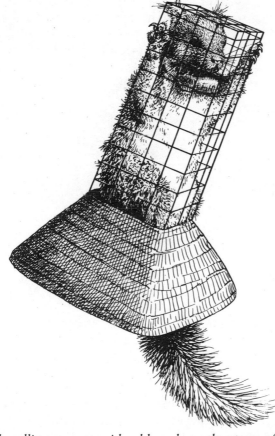

A wire mesh handling cone considerably reduces the stress of holding a squirrel, both for animal and biologist.

Tame squirrels will allow themselves to be touched, particularly if the approaching hand bears some food. They will also perform cute tricks like climbing up your trousers or jumper, and perching on your shoulder. This actually hurts, as they have very sharp claws that have to dig into you to get a grip. However, squirrels do not like to be squeezed, and you can very easily kill one by mishandling it.

In the case of unco-operative squirrels that need to be handled – say, to extricate them from some difficulty – you are best advised to wear a stiff pair of gloves for the job. Don't grip the squirrel around its chest or abdomen, or it may go into a kind of shock faint, and can even succumb completely. It is best to make a ring with the thumb and forefinger of your left hand around the animal's neck, not throttling it, but just supporting it. Then lift it up, catch the squirrel's front leg between the fore and middle finger of the same hand, and support its weight on its armpit. Your hold should be firm, but, whatever you do, don't squeeze.

Handle with care and DO NOT SQUEEZE.

For the purpose of weighing and measuring squirrels under study, you can avoid all the palaver of handling the animal (and the risk of getting bitten) if you use a wire mesh handling cone. This piece of equipment is shaped like a wire Smartie tube, the right size for the squirrel to get into, but too small for it to turn round. One end is blocked off, and the other end has a special hook to close it. Once inside here, the squirrel cannot damage itself, it cannot bite you, and it is not subject to the stress of being held. I must admit, I swear by them, and I've never heard a squirrel complain about the arrangement.

Methods of marking squirrels

It is a shame that, unlike periwinkles, tortoises, hedgehogs, and other conveniently slow animals, it is impossible for you to mark a squirrel without getting hold of it and somehow pinning it down. And for that you need a licence (see p.123).

It is possible to get these licences for scientific study, and then you can devise ways of catching and marking squirrels so that you can tell them apart. One of the standard ways of marking mammals is by clipping an identification mark into their fur. This mark can then be checked every time the animal is caught, and, with a lot of luck, could possibly be read through a pair of binoculars at a distance (but not very easily because the squirrel always sits on the bit you need to see). There is a problem, though. Squirrels moult their fur twice a year, and the mark will disappear with each moult. So you would have to continually replace it. There is also the problem of the one who disappears for a while, and then returns to your study area. You will mark him as a new animal because he doesn't carry a mark, but he is in fact an old acquaintance that has moulted. For a short-term study, fur clipping is ideal, but it isn't really any good in the long term. The same goes for fur dying too.

How else can you mark your squirrel? Various colour coded collars and ear tags have been used. Some are very effective and can be easily read at a distance as well as in the hand. The only problem is that squirrels do have a habit of losing their tags, and then you are stuck with the same problem as you had with the one who slipped off for a quick moult. Is it a new animal or an old one who has removed his tag? At least with an ear tag there would be a small hole in the squirrel's ear to tell you he'd been caught before. But no clue as to exactly who he is.

Radio tagging is the most high-tech way to mark a squirrel. You know exactly which one it is because the transmitters all have different frequencies. You have the additional advantage that the tag is actually useful, as it allows you to find the squrirel whenever you want to. However, the price of radio tags is enough to put most people off. Alternatively, you could always give them names!

Red squirrel conservation: a case for looking after the habitat

We are all aware of the gradual disappearance of our native red squirrels. So much so, that we have scheduled them as an endangered species. But what are we actually doing about it? I am afraid that the answer is really not a lot. Believe it or not, we are still at the research stage: finding out exactly what it is that these beasties need in order to thrive and breed. We still don't know what the problems are between red and grey squirrels, although we are just starting to make tentative suggestions as to what might be going on. It is certainly a bit premature to start making sweeping suggestions about what we could do to conserve red squirrels. However, we've got to do something, or else we might find ourselves without a problem at all — no squirrels to save.

All sorts of management techniques are under investigation, like selective feeding of reds to improve their survival and breeding success. Provision of weight-selective boxes either for nesting, or as hoppers containing food for reds only, is another possible cushion against a rapid takeover by greys. However, these devices can sometimes be fooled by clever grey squirrels which learn to gain entry by keeping their full weight off the trigger mechanism at the entrance. In the long term, if grey squirrels are exerting an influence over reds purely by being there (say, by suppression of red squirrel breeding in response to the inevitable rise in population density, by exerting social pressures in conjunction with overcrowding or by simply gobbling up all the grub), red squirrel conservation without the control of grey squirrels would be impractical.

It would appear that one of the most sensible ways in which we could seek to manage surviving red squirrel populations is by understanding their habitat requirements. By ensuring conservation of the very best bits of squirrel habitat, you are inadvertently doing a lot for the squirrels that live in them. This is why it is so vital for us to understand exactly what sort of woodland red squirrels like best.

According to recent studies, red squirrels are just as happy in either pure conifer forest, in a mixture of broadleaved and conifer, or in pure broadleaved woodland. So that's not much help. The best thing would be to further these studies by looking at population levels in woods containing different combinations of tree species and ages to see what is most successful. On the Isle of Wight, I have been looking at broadleaved woodland types, particularly old native woods, to see which red squirrels prefer. They seem to do best in woods containing old oak and ash trees, with plenty of other species mixed in, like field maple and hornbeam. These provide a variety of foods at different times of the year. A coppiced understorey of hazel provides the most valuable squirrel food source, although care must be taken when planning the coppice rotation. Red squirrels at my study sites actively avoided newly coppiced and young stools. There simply wasn't enough cover for them. They preferred to forage in the older nut-bearing hazel, especially when there were some large old trees left standing amongst the coppice, or the whole belt was situated alongside some full grown timber. The best coppice rotation for red squirrels would be about 15 or 20 years for each cut, but always making sure that there are interlacing areas of older overgrown coppice within the wood. This way, there is always plenty of good squirrel habitat despite that fact that the wood is being worked.

In the case of conifer woodland, red squirrels make good use of Scots pine, larch, fir and spruce trees once they have reached cone-bearing age. This means that for squirrels, the best conifer woodland is mature — just at the stage when it is most useless to virtually all other wildlife, with nothing growing on the ground because of the complete shade cast by a thick, dark canopy. This presents a problem for the conservationist, not least because recent research increasingly points towards conifer woodlands as the only realistic home for red squirrels in the future.

Studies of reds and greys living in similar deciduous woodlands have shown that grey squirrels are at a distinct competitive advantage in this habitat (see p.22). With a variety of tree species and their seeds as a food supply, red squirrels concentrate their foraging efforts on hazel nuts, even when there are thousands of acorns available. This appears to be because red squirrels cannot digest acorns very efficiently. As a result, reds spend very little time on the ground. They feed up in the tree canopy on ripening hazels, and although they do come down to the ground to cache some of them, they are often aloft throughout the winter feeding on fungi like *Vuillemenia* (see p.75 & 92) instead of eating stored seeds.

Grey squirrels on the other hand make full use of the abundant acorn crop. They spend much of their time on the ground feeding on stored seeds, which they can digest far more efficiently than the reds. This gives them the competitive edge when the two species co-exist in broadleaved woodland because greys can spend a larger proportion of the year feeding on high-energy tree seeds than reds. The result is that greys breed more successfully, and that their young have a better chance of survival. As we have already discussed (see p.105) this results in higher grey squirrel density. Now imagine the two species in the same woodland. The greys polish off the red squirrel's preferred hazel crop in a matter of days, leaving the reds with no choice but to feed on acorns which they cannot even digest properly. Small wonder that they do not thrive.

The silver lining to this rather black cloud is that in coniferous woodland, the boot might just be on the other foot. Red squirrels are well adapted to a life up in the tops of conifer trees feeding on cone seed, and in this case, greys do not have as much evolutionary experience. As we have just described, the heavier grey is a broadleaved woodland specialist, and it appears that whilst they can certainly make do in coniferous woodland, they do not thrive quite as disgustingly well! With the two species more evenly matched, there is a chance that our native squirrel might just be able to hold its own against the grey invader; and this is where research is turning now. In the future, we may be able to look to coniferous woodland as a conservation resource for red squirrels. The trouble is that it is not much of a conservation resource for anything else. What's more, the fact that greys can use acorns so much more efficiently than reds means that livening up a dull conifer plantation with a few oaks could spell disaster for the resident reds and actually accelerate the invasion of their refuge by greys.

Since coniferous woodland is about the only habitat type that has actually grown in acreage during recent years, it would be good to look upon it as a constructive future refuge for reds. However, it must be said that I am sure the thousands of hectares of planted coniferous habitat that we now have are ample for the purposes of conserving a few squirrels. We certainly don't need any more! We're also going to need some innovative management techniques, some brave new ideas to try and improve these red squirrel islands for other wildlife. I have no doubt that, given the will and the cash, anything is possible.

And one last plea. If you are lucky enough to live on an island and can protect your red squirrels from invasion by greys, better to pick a native broadleaved wood as your squirrel conservation area any day.

Re-introductions

There is no doubt that the concept of re-introduction is extremely creative. If, for one reason or another, a species is forced into extinction in a particular area, it may be re-instated at a later date should the prevailing circumstances once again favour its survival, by re-introduction. Indeed, zoos and other wildlife collections may provide a valuable service to conservation by captive breeding, thereby securing stocks of endangered animals threatened in the wild. These sheltered and protected stocks may then be utilized in carefully planned re-introduction programmes to restore, once again, the wild populations. As many of you will be aware, red squirrels have been the subject of re-introduction programmes over the past few years, notably at Regent's Park in London (although others have been proposed). What is the wisdom behind these plans, and what chance do they have of success?

Obviously before such projects are undertaken, it is essential to consider carefully their likelihood of success. Bodies like the International Union for the Conservation of Nature (IUCN) have drawn up guidelines for proposed re-introductions. For a start it is recommended that you should know as much as possible about the ecology and physiology of the species concerned. Basically, the more that you know about the animal, the more likely you are to be able to identify its problems, and understand its initial extinction. Armed with a thorough knowledge of red and grey squirrels, we should be able to work out if and how they affect one another directly, and maybe even identify ways in which we could intervene to the red squirrel's advantage. Modern research techniques are improving scientific understanding of squirrels all the time, but we're still learning about the basic ecology of the two species, and are a long way from understanding their relationship with one another.

Secondly, the IUCN recommends that one should determine why it is that the species in question disappeared from the place where it is to be re-introduced in the first place. As we have discussed, there are all sorts of reasons given for the red squirrel's demise. These include aggression between the two species, disease problems, and the suggestion that ecological competition (say for food, nest sites or space) might occur between reds and greys. The problem of aggression has been researched, and could not account for the replacement of reds by greys. However, neither the question of disease, nor ecological competition is at all well understood. In other words, we cannot possibly claim to understand why red squirrels have been replaced by greys yet, and thus are in no position to assess whether conditions at our proposed re-introduction site now favour survival of our released red squirrels.

The Regent's Park re-introduction set out to investigate whether supplementary feeding of red squirrels only might improve their chances of survival in the face of competition from the grey. Red squirrels were fed from weight-selective hoppers, which only admitted the lighter squirrel and not its heavier cousin (mind you, the odd grey found out how to swindle the hoppers by balancing with only front paws on the treadle mechanism!). It would be interesting to know what they discovered, but certainly my own research into the effects of supplementary feeding on wild red squirrels is very disappointing. The extra rations do not seem to make much difference at all. Unlike greys, which can become quite obese with regular feeding, my study reds did not get any fatter than their unfed neighbours. They did not produce any more babies, although those that they did produce tended to come earlier in the year that those of the unfed squirrels. They still moved about as much, and were just as vulnerable to bad weather and natural food shortage. So it would seem that supplementary feeding alone would just not be enough.

Thirdly, the guidelines advise that one make sure that the re-introduced species's niche has not been filled by another species during its absence. This is the real crunch for red squirrels. Of course, their niche has been ably filled by grey squirrels. As far as we understand at the moment, the only chance that reds would have of re-establishing themselves would have to involve complete and maintained removal of grey squirrels. In most cases, this would be impractical even if it was considered desirable.

Apart from these factors, one also has to take into account a whole host of other considerations. There is the welfare of the squirrels. Red squirrels are protected by law, so it is illegal to disturb them, let alone catch and move them. You would need a licence to do that. If red squirrels are to be re-introduced to a suitable site, they would have to come from somewhere. The IUCN recommends that one should be quite sure that removal of individuals does no harm to the source population. In the case of the Regent's Park re-introduction, the red squirrels involved were removed from a private estate in Fife where they had been causing damage to trees. If they had not been taken to London, they would most probably have been killed. Perhaps it would be a good idea to use any future such waifs to populate a captive breeding programme, which might serve re-introductions in the future should research ever show that the venture were likely to be successful.

Maybe Britain just isn't a good place for red squirrels to live for climatic reasons. They are at the edge of their natural range here anyway and the fragmented, modified nature of most modern woodlands and countryside just isn't suitable. Perhaps *they* made a mistake coming here in the first place after the last Ice Age and we might be making another in trying to re-establish them – at least in the south. We should think a lot about issues like this before acting precipitately.

In short, the idea of reintroductions involves a whole lot more than just letting a few squirrels go in your local park. I personally feel that re-introductions are going to play an increasingly important part in our positive and creative conservation plans for the future. However, I think that in the case of red squirrels, there is still so much more that we need to understand before we could possibly be justified in going ahead. What is the point in spending huge amounts of time, energy and money, not to mention putting the squirrels through unnecessary suffering, unless you are very sure that the exercise is going to be a success? We really have to understand the red/grey problems before turning to re-introductions of red squirrels.

Apart from anything else, re-introducing species is a controversial act, and one that is likely to stir deep feelings amongst all sorts of people. All the more reason that the first projects should be 'watertight', and a more or less guaranteed success. Re-introducing red squirrels just seems to me to be too much of a shot in the dark yet. Why spoil the potential of a useful technique by launching into the first projects without having done your homework?

Squirrels as pests

Squirrels are quite notorious as pests, although often the damage they do is merely irritating. They will get under your roof tiles and build extravagant nests in your loft. Not a major misdemeanour, but quite alarming to anybody dozing in the bedroom below; mammoths have nothing on a squirrel rampant in the loft. They steal things, too. I have actually witnessed a grey squirrel stealing eggs from a hen house. Naughty, I know, but it was absolutely fascinating to watch how the animal coped with a package so evidently not designed for carrying up trees under one's chin.

THERE IT IS AGAIN, HAROLD... ...LISTEN..

The folk who really regard squirrels as pests are our foresters. There is no doubt that squirrels do damage commercially valuable trees by stripping their bark in order to get at the sweet sap below. But are they really serious pests? The answer is that it depends who you are. If you are trying to grow young beech and sycamore trees, then yes, they are pests. Certainly a great deal of effort is expended in squirrel control. Red squirrels are now legally protected, and thus anyone suffering the ravages of bark-stripping reds would have to apply for a licence to take counter measures. Grey squirrels are classed as vermin; they do not enjoy the luxury of such protection. In most commercial woods they are heavily culled to prevent damage before it occurs.

Ways of killing squirrels

What an unpleasant thought. People use a number of different methods for killing squirrels, some more controversial than others. During the 1800s, and in some parts even into this century, landlords would pay a bounty of a shilling-a-tail for squirrels. This bounty system was a pretty ineffective control incentive. Any gamekeeper worth his salt would just get all his mates to send him tails, no matter where from, instead of wasting his own energy leaping about the place trying to kill squirrels. So the poor old Lord of the Manor was simply paying through the nose for somebody else's tails.

Modern squirrel control is often piecemeal, and directed at grey squirrels. Gamekeepers and foresters go out for a bit of sport shooting greys, or partaking of the traditional drey poking and shooting. These methods account for a fairly insignificant number of squirrels each year, and probably have little effect on the population levels. Traps are also used. Either multi-capture cage traps in which the captured squirrel or squirrels are later killed, or spring traps that kill the animal outright. Whilst studying grey squirrels in commercial forests, it was not unknown to see three-legged

animals bearing the scars of a near miss with one of these traps. Indeed, one female I recall had actually gone on to breed and raise a family despite the loss of her limb.

Poisoning with Warfarin is becoming an increasingly popular method of killing squirrels. The problem is that in order to get your intended victim, you have to leave poisoned bait lying about in hoppers. It is inevitable that other wildlife will eat a fair amount of the doctored squirrel grub. It has been suggested that poison hoppers should be placed on tables, out of harm's way, rather than on the ground and that putting poison on certain baits that squirrels like best would minimize the toll amongst other wildlife. However, even so this method would leave lethal doses of mammal killer lying about in the countryside. And if squirrels can get at it, then surely so can countless other things.

Squirrel tales

Squirrels may well delight the majority of people these days, but they have not always been as popular. In days gone by, despite the fact that people were kept busy simply surviving, they still found time to mythologize about wildlife. The squirrel's habit of chattering and scolding from some vantage out of reach was interpreted as a sign of mischief. Squirrels were thought to be trouble-makers, and even accused of being responsible for accidents and bad happenings. I have read that they were said to run the gauntlet between 'evil' in the roots of a tree, and 'good' in the crown. Presumably this image was derived from their frequent passage to and from the tree canopy, spiralling up or down the trunk in an effortless glide. Squirrels were believed to enjoy the protection of Thor himself, the God of thunder. One would hardly credit such an inoffensive little beast with such extraordinary powers.

Considering that the squirrel had been given such awesome and sinister connections in the deep and darkest past, it is hard to see how it could have been transformed to delight millions of small children as Tufty Squirrel, or the adorable Squirrel Nutkin. Personally I think that the squirrel's character and general demeanour suits these labels far better than the bedevilled bringer of evil and bad luck. Indeed, so far improved has been the squirrel's image recently that one Tufty was actually used in order to encourage small children to be careful on our modern roads (he has since been banned for some obscure social reason).

By far the most charming of our children's squirrel stories is that told by the inimitable Beatrix Potter in her Squirrel Nutkin tales. Surely everyone remembers the drawings of a fleet of little red squirrels sailing across a lake on rafts, with their fluffy tails held aloft like sails to catch the breeze. It might seem far-fetched, but this picture was not only in Beatrix Potter's mind. I have found reference to the sailing antics of red squirrels in quite serious zoological texts, including one of some considerable antiquity, written in the seventeenth century. Mind you, the same text also contained learned chapters on the biology of dragons, demons and centaurs. It is fascinating to speculate where the original sailing squirrel story came from. Certainly squirrels do cross water, and I suppose that one hitching a ride on a piece of driftwood could conceivably be interpreted as using a raft. Squirrels often hold their tails erect, making them look rather like sails or flags. They even make group migrations on occasion. But quite how one would explain the picnic that they are said to carry with them, in case some unscheduled mishap should befall them upon their journey, I cannot imagine.

Once a story has been told, it is easy to see how it can be perpetuated. Passed down from generations of storytellers, usually with some considerable embroidery and enlargement. And finally you have yourself a fully fledged legend. Perhaps that is how the myth that squirrels hibernate has managed to survive for so long. Somebody suggested it once upon a time, and it has been faithfully and incorrectly repeated through the generations ever since.

Squirrel studies

It is very difficult to suggest projects studying squirrels that you could do yourself. Most useful ideas require that you should be able to tell individual squirrels apart, and of course you can't do that without catching and marking the animals. That requires skill, equipment and, in the case of red squirrels, a licence. However, I have got a couple of suggestions, and would be delighted to hear of the results.

Firstly, and quite simply, you might like to look at your garden squirrels' preferences for different foods. You could do this by placing weighed amounts of different foods out where the squirrels normally visit. At the end of the day, you weigh the leftovers, and see what the list of favourites was. You would, of course need to repeat the exercise on a number of separate occasions, and also take care of a few problems. For a start, it's no good if all the neighbourhood birds come and tuck into your samples. So you'd either have to watch and make sure only the squirrels visited your food, or you could teach the squirrels to use some sort of a hopper that only they could gain access to. Squirrels are quite smart, and can soon be taught to press a lever in return for a food reward. I've actually seen film of an American grey squirrel that had learned how to operate a vending machine selling chocolate, without putting in any money. Mind you, he went for the same selection each time; probably the chocolate bar with the most nuts in it. Once the squirrel is trigger happy, just offer him a series of hoppers with different foods, and see which once he visits the most. You'd certainly know what to feed him during hard times.

Another idea is to try and keep an eye on the condition of your local squirrels throughout the year, so that you could time your supplementary feeding more precisely. I have recently had considerable success using a baited bird table, placed on top of some postal scales, so that I could weigh the squirrels when they come to feed. For the purposes of my research, this rather Heath Robinson affair has now been replaced by an electric digital balance where the weight is displayed as illuminated numbers; soon it will be computerized and automated.

What you do is to get hold of some scales that weigh between 0–800g. In practice this is virtually impossible, so I settled for postal scales that measure up to 1Kg, but are quite accurate below 500g. for the purpose of weighing letters. Don't use a pan on top, but instead, attach a light plywood board, about 15–18 inches long, and 12 inches wide. You will probably need to glue the two together, as otherwise the squirrels will be forever

tipping bait all over themselves. Place the scales and their table where you normally feed, preferably within easy sight of a convenient window in your house, say on top of a sturdy bird table. Make sure that the squirrels have some way of easily getting onto the plywood board, but don't lean things against it. Put your squirrel food on the board at a set time each day, so that they get used to coming at a certain time. Then just sit back in your armchair with a pair of binoculars and record their weights when they visit. You should expect a healthy adult red squirrel to weigh about 250–270g. (8–9½oz.) in the summer, and 290–320g. (10–11oz.) in the autumn and winter. For a grey, about 500–550g. (17½–19½oz.) in the summer, and 650–700g. (23–24½oz.) in the winter months. Youngsters are a bit lighter in both cases. What you should look out for are exceptionally light animals during the spring and summer that might benefit from some extra rations. Happy squirrel watching.

Squirrels and the law

Red and grey squirrels are treated differently by British Law. Since 1981, and the advent of the new Wildlife and Countryside Act, red squirrels have been recognized as one of our rarer mammals, and are consequently protected. You should not disturb or harm a red squirrel, or its nest, and you need a special licence should you need to catch one for any reason. Grey squirrels, on the other hand, are classed with the 'vermin', animals that you are allowed to catch and kill, but which you must not release into the wild.

The Act requires that people like myself, who study red squirrels, are licensed; that licence is obtainable from the Nature Conservancy Council upon receipt of a jolly good reason for wanting to catch, mark or otherwise disturb the beasts. That's not the end of it either. You will be expected to provide information to show that your study has been valid, and, should this prove unsatisfactory, your licence will be withdrawn. The same goes for forestry organizations that might want to control red squirrels causing damage to trees. They must now apply for a licence, which may not be granted if red squirrels are otherwise scarce in their area. To kill the squirrels without a licence is a prosecutable offence, and could lead to a hefty fine. However, as we have seen (see p.114), in the only case of such an application to control red squirrels for forestry purposes, a solution was found that kept both squirrels and foresters happy.

If you have any problems or queries regarding squirrels and the law, it is best to get in touch with your local Nature Conservancy Council Office and ask their advice.

Further information

If you would like to delve into things 'squirrel' in greater depth, and read around this subject more extensively, these titles might be of use to you. Monica Shorten's account of both red and grey squirrels is still superb value, and well worth a read. Her monograph *Squirrels* was published in the Collins New Naturalist series in 1954, and, if you can manage to get hold of a copy (it is now out of print), I strongly recommend it. It is a comprehensive book, and yet is very easy to read, with particularly good chapters on the history of squirrels in Britain. Another very comprehensive text is that of John Gurnell's book *The Natural History of Squirrels* (March, 1987) in the Christopher Helm mammal series. This book draws together much of the more modern scientific thinking and research on squirrels, both here in Britain, and also further afield in Europe and America. If you were to read these two texts, you could safely say that you knew about as much on the subject of squirrels as the rest of us do.

Other useful accounts of squirrels have been published in the *Handbook of British Mammals* edited by Southern and Corbet (Blackwell, 1984), with chapters on both species. The *Encyclopedia of Mammals*, edited by David Macdonald (Guild Publishing, 1985), has some lovely photographs of all sorts of different squirrels, excellent sections on foreign squirrels, and the problems of squirrel bark stripping. For the younger reader, Andrew Tittensor has published a book in association with the Mammal Society all about red squirrels, and Keith Laidler's book *Squirrels in Britain* published by David and Charles (1980) contains some nice photographs which might inspire the young enthusiast to read on.

Useful addresses

The Mammal Society
c/o The Linnean Society
Burlington House
Piccadilly
London W1V 0LQ

Mammal Society Publications
Miss R Harper at above address

Ministry of Agriculture Fisheries and Food
Veterinary Investigation Centre
Government Buildings
Jupiter Road
Norwich
Norfolk NR6 6ST

Ministry of Agriculture Fisheries and Food
Mammal Section
Alice Holt Research Section
Farnham
Surrey

The Fauna and Flora Preservation Society
c/o Zoological Society of London
Regent's Park
London NW1 4RY

Nature Conservancy Council
Northminster House
Peterborough PE1 5UA

Squirrel food:
Duffetts of Ryde
Corn Merchants
High Street
Ryde
Isle of Wight

Index